W9-CZU-896

NEO-CATECHUMENAL
COMMUNITIES

RICARDO BLÁZQUEZ

NEO-CATECHUMENAL COMMUNITIES

A theological discernment

 **St Paul Publications**

Original title: *Le comunità Neo-Catecumenali. Discernimento teologico*. Copyright © Edizioni Paoline s.r.l., Cinisello Balsamo (Italy), 1987.

Translated by Peter Corbishley
Icon by Kiko Argüello
Cover design by Mary Lou Winters, fsp

St Paul Publications
Middlegreen, Slough SL3 6BT, England

English translation © St Paul Publications 1988
Printed by Hollen Street Press, Slough
ISBN 085439 280 7

St Paul Publications is an activity of the priests and brothers of the Society of St Paul who proclaim the Gospel through the media of social communication.

CONTENTS

INTRODUCTION

The Neo-Catechumenal Way, the journey of Christian initiation followed by Neo-Catechumenal communities, is not the result of a piece of pastoral planning. Rather its origin shows all the hallmarks of being a precious gift of God. It began in 1964 in the shanty town of Palomeras Altas on the outskirts of Madrid with Francisco Argüello, a painter, otherwise known as Kiko. He had been converted to Christian faith from an existentialist type of atheism, and went to the shanty town taking a bible, a crucifix and a guitar. His intention, following the inspiration of Charles de Foucauld, was to live silently, a poor man among the poor. He soon became a question mark for those around who asked him to talk to them about Jesus Christ. He was taken by surprise happy to find that a profound bond of fraternity grew up there among the Gypsies who came to his shanty to listen to his improvised catecheses. Kiko

---

*The present work is an updated revision of what originally appeared in *Teología y Cataquesis* 4 (1984) 603-641.

remembers with wonder how the kerygma, in so far as it was accepted by these poor people, created communion.

So in the shanty town, under the presidency of a presbyter known to Kiko, the Eucharist began to be celebrated with such simplicity and power that the experience spread rapidly. This was the seed. As always in Christianity, the living reality comes first, followed by reflection and eventually organization. Peter, and those faithful who were circumcised, are astonished to see that the gift of the Holy Spirit is also poured out on the Gentiles (cf Ac 10:44-45; 11:11-18). And Paul sees the power of the Word of God regenerating the lives of those who welcome it before he calls his communities the 'body of Christ'.

Overwhelmed with the reality which was growing up Kiko and Carmen (a member of a religious Institute who on the way from Madrid to Bolivia had been highly impressed by what she had seen happening at Palomeras) understood one thing: what had been given by God had to be made freely available. They agreed to requests coming from several parishes to give the catecheses which had given rise to the first community. This was the beginning of the growth of the Neo-Catechumenal Way which, at present, has spread to more than eighty countries throughout the five continents. The Way is always accompanied by signs given by God and interpretable by those who are open to the Spirit. The two initiators understood, too, that they were responsible for a gift coming from God: a task put into their trust for the service of the Church and mankind. They realized, therefore, that the Way has to be followed unconditionally. It has to be kept carefully in its originality and jealously defended.

Several of the foundational realities of Christianity are at the core of the Neo-Catechumenal Way. These are the annunciation of the resurrection of Jesus Christ, the Servant of God as the meaning of that cross which everyone has, the rediscovery of baptism as a goal, and the Catechumenate as a way of conversion and of faith. All these are related to the experience of the pioneer community, which has has been deepened and clarified with history, theology, liturgy and spirituality. Everything is done with attention fixed on the direction of the bishops and particularly the Bishop of Rome. The initiators, on the one hand, are persuaded – and in this they have been confirmed by ecclesiastical authority – that they have received a charism from God for the postconciliar Church. On the other hand, they are open to the signs through which God is showing how the charism might finally be shaped and incardinated within the Church. In every context – as with the presentation of their Way which is the subject of this book – they submit themselves loyally to the sieve of ecclesial discernment. In doing so they appeal to that truth of the Gospel in which the worth of a plant is judged by its fruits. There is much, then, to be gained by comparing the development of the Neo-Catechumenal Way with the origins and statements of other great reform movements in the Church.[1]

The Neo-Catechumenal Way brings together the totality of Christianity in an original synthesis. As it unfolds, every Christian reality receives its own particular emphasis while being progressively reintegrated into the whole. For over ten years while I have been part of a community and as someone with an on-going interest in its theological dimension I have been frequently surprised by its coherence, depth and originality. The way is the coherent disclosure of a deeply profound intuition. Faced with its 'novelty' one needs both calm reflection and the help of the Christian techniques of discernment. One needs that freedom of spirit which is primarily concerned with the underlying reality. Such a spirit is not put off by a less than happy phraseology, rather it particularly takes account of the strongly 'kerygmatic' tone of the words. The consequent awakening is such as to push one on to further questions, further searching, and further understanding.

The Neo-Catechumenal Way is a post-conciliar initiative. It always presupposes the Council. It is based on the liturgical, biblical and ecclesiological renewal assumed and promulgated by the Council. But its own newness lies in a creative genius which brings all this together in a dynamic affinity. A theoretical grasp of all the elements is insufficient. Reformed rituals, a rich biblical learning, the best catechetical theory, a renewed conceptualization of the Church can all co-exist without much in the way of life. A creative genius, however, brings all the elements together in an original way, forming a living and fruitful unity.

I will outline the Neo-Catechumenal Way under three of its aspects. Firstly I will collect together the major insights from which it springs. Then I shall describe how it has actually taken shape. Finally I will put down some thoughts as to how, from the point of view of the Neo-Catechumenal Way, its acceptance might be encouraged.

I

THE MAJOR FOUNDATIONAL
INSPIRATIONS

Nothing is further from the Neo-Catechumenal Way than a determination to depend
upon techniques derived from either psychology or sociology for the formation of
community. Group dynamics, strategies for
personal integration, the fostering of 'warm'
relationships and so on, are not directly
sought as such. The steadfastness of community comes from its deepest experiences.
When these have been shared, vitally and in

good measure by its members, they yield an unforgettable impact and form an indestructible bond. To judge from its continuance, they are the source of a truly remarkable cohesiveness. When compared with the countless initiatives which melt away like the summer mist such persistence of itself raises its own question mark. The rich nourishment found in the Neo-Catechumenal communities is shown by the fact that people come twice weekly, year after year. They come completely free, gently drawn in as a result of a kindliness felt a thousand times over. Suitably prepared celebrations release an energy which has the power to nourish and prompt the way of faith and conversion among the participants. The community does not meet to focus on study or discussion, or to plan events, programmes or campaigns. It meets primarily to celebrate the Word of God and the Eucharist. And it is through these last two, in fact, that the journey is routed.

THE RESURRECTION OF JESUS CHRIST
IS ANNOUNCED

It is essential to proclaim the kerygma of the Resurrection in as many ways as possible during the first stage which is the formation of community. Communion arises only in so far as this good news is welcomed. And all the remaining development of community will be shot through with the announcement of the kerygma. God makes a promise of salvation to people in their own situation. So everyone needs to discover personally what that is for them. In the name of the Church, the catechists assure their hearers that God will faithfully bring this promise to fulfilment. This promise is such that in so far as it comes to be believed we are kept moving. The announcement of the resurrection accepted in the power of the Spirit begins to work for our salvation. Preaching the kerygma is a free offering of the Gospel. It is the hope that comes from God for the unredeemed. The Good News pours out from the heart of a God who loves each individual whatever the circumstances of his life. It is a message which does not come to judge or to condemn. It does not come to make demands on us in our weakness. Yet it has more power to recreate us than all proscriptions and injunctions. One cannot be renewed without the prior experience of a freely given love. New life is possible only in so far as a new man is coming into being, clothed in Jesus Christ. Christian morality is a response. God's grace comes before one's duty. We reply to a divine initiative. The imprint of God's work precedes the exhortations and imperatives of our action. One thinks, for example, of the letters of St Paul. To go forward on an opposite basis is moralism. This is put so clearly in the Neo-Catechumenal Way that the emphasis on God's gratuitousness and on the incapacity of our strength raises a degree of anxiety among some at the beginning of the way. At the beginning all that is asked is that one listens to the Word of God. So that, little by little, one is made ready to grasp and respond to the many other Christian demands. It is clearly recognized that human freedom is, as if it were, in chains.

The proclamation of the Resurrection is addressed to us, people enslaved through the fear of death. This brings us to one of the most central issues. According to Hebrews 2:14-15 we are held in slavery for the whole of our lives through the fear we have of death. If we are not made fully aware of this human circumstance the kerygma cannot develop its full impact. Everyone of us as we sin undergoes an experience of death. Existentially we taste what sin leads to. Sin destroys man from within. It does not somehow simply remain on the outside. If this dimension of sin is not fully grasped sin remains something extrinsic. It will seem to relate only to our relations with the outside, with God, other people, or the world. But sin, on this view, leaves our intimate reality untouched. In addition sin creates a deadly boundary which encircles everyone of us. Man is a prisoner within this circle from which he cannot escape on his own. Everyone of us is unable to open up to other people; we cannot reach out and transcend ourselves in the other person; the experience of death which possesses us stops us loving at the moment when someone else is felt to be 'destroying', 'killing' and repressing. We continue to love only in so far as the person who is the focus of love is being affirmative. We want to love in a different way but we are held back from within ourselves and remain slaves. If this situation is not broken out of we cannot fulfil the law of God. And all threats and warnings remain sterile.

In this kerygmatic phase the narrative of

Genesis 3, the fall of Adam and Eve, you and I, is headlined eloquently and concretely. Adam and Eve believe in the catechesis of the devil: 'You will be like gods' (Gn 3:5); God's prohibition is due to his jealousy in the face of the potential grandeur of man; God has imposed the law on you because he fears you; he does not love you; it is to limit your freedom and to entrap your fulfilment. They eat the forbidden fruit. They say 'yes' to the 'serpent'. They deny that God is love. At the root of every sin there is this thrust to atheism, to deceit, to murder (cf Gn 8:31ff). Sinning brings with it an experience of death, of deprivation, of separation, and a sense of guilt. Sin gives birth to death; it leads neither to freedom nor to human improvement. For us all, life comes from obedience to God. If we reject God our life loses its meaning. For we are alive only in so far as God gives us our being out of love. Here is the root of the evil in us; from then on it is as if we, sold into sin, do the evil that we have no desire for (Rm 7:14ff). Sin has repaid us with death, for 'the wages of sin is death' (Rm 6:23). 'Once, when there was no Law, I was alive; but when the commandment came, sin came to life and I died' (Rm 7:9). This is the source of all our troubles, all our suffering. A grasp of this truth about our existential situation means that the grace of God in the dead and risen

Jesus Christ reaches to the innermost depths of our unredemption. Christ is the new Adam. God's revelation in Jesus brings out our profound reality as both the abyss of downfall and the grandeur of salvation. And so we can see that to understand our reality primarily in social and collective terms leaves out an essential aspect of Christian reality. At any rate what the Neo-Catechumenal communities say hits upon this profound reality. If this core is illuminated by the Word of God, if it is touched by the liberation of the Spirit of Jesus, an individual is radically saved. One can be enjoying the best of health, living in abundance and revelling in all that life can offer but live with a deadly emptiness within if this deep point is not brought into consideration and purified. And so we see that in our society the sting of this existential death is not drawn, but takes even greater hold.

The kerygma of the Resurrection of Jesus resounds as a joyous, good news in our existential situation, enslaved by the fear of death. Life is possible! Life is freely offered to you here and now! Christianity fundamentally consists in this good news. Jesus's preaching was a good news (cf Mk 1:14), as was that of the apostles (cf Ac 5:42). Jesus Christ has broken the circle of death and sin which oppresses us and closes off the path to liberty. Jesus Christ has conquered 'the lord of death' (cf Heb 2:14). So thus freed we can pass through the barrier which separates us from the others and love them. Death has been swallowed up in victory (cf 1 Cor 15:54-57). Christian love is born in the one who is freed from the fear of death. It is a love to the death, love in the dimension of the cross, love for the enemy (cf Jn 15:12-13; Mt 5:43-48). This is the way Jesus loved. This is how God loved us when we were sinners (cf Rm 5:6-11). In Jesus Christ, conqueror of death, and through his resurrection everything that bears the mark of death is overcome. This is not to talk simply of the guarantee of final resurrection, to the after-life. There is also the power of new life at the centre of our existence overladen with precariousness, pain, the cross, everything that represses us. In the life of the Christian there is a glorious inversion of death through the power of the Spirit who raised Jesus from death. In liberty and triumph, in joy and gratitude, every Christian can call out, along with St Paul, 'Death where is your victory? Death where is your sting? The sting of death is sin and the power of sin comes from the Law. We give thanks to God who gives us the victory through our Lord Jesus Christ!' (1 Cor 15:55-57). Pauline exegesis shows that there is a parallel between Genesis 3 and the victory of Jesus Christ over the Law, sin and death. Paul's theology is the key for the understanding of the Neo-Catechumenal communities. Paul concentrates powerfully upon the death and resurrection of Jesus Christ. He emphasizes the existential power of sin and the superabundant power of grace. He insists upon the cross, upon faith, upon graciousness and upon the role of the Spirit in the new existence. These are also the emphases of the Neo-Catechumenal Way. Obviously to stress one aspect is not to say that others are to be excluded. But the emphases determine the overall framework. They create the particular characteristics. They shape its strengths and weaknesses.

God freely offers us his achievement, Jesus Christ dead and risen, so that our sins may be destroyed and our death annihilated. Jesus is the way that God has opened into death. We can all pass from death to life through the power of the Holy Spirit. God has done this and in so doing has shown us his love. The serpent has no grounds on which to present God to us as our enemy. Our life lies in obedience to the will of God, our death and destruction in the disobedience of sin.

God loved us because we were suffering and destroyed, slaves and sinners. We are prisoners more than sinners. This is the intuition which is profoundly Christian. An exclu-

sively ethical perspective on sin has sometimes stopped us from grasping its theological and existential dimension. Jesus will
reproach the Pharisees for their justice,
which is based on carrying out the Law, and
found wanting by God. He will plead for
sinners because they are tired from the
weight. God has had pity on us and has
stretched out his hand to us in Jesus Christ.
This, not the one suggested by the Tempter,
is the true face of God. It is what Romans
5:6-11 says about the radical goodness of
God's initiative shown to us in the actions of
Jesus Christ.

Historico-critical research verifies that this
is the characteristic behaviour of Jesus towards sinners, the poor, the ignorant and the
needy. Jesus changed the relationship between penitence and salvation which ruled
in the Judaism of his time. For Jesus conversion springs from grace. The hope for all
those whose life is destroyed is the fact that
God is good and opens the way to life in the
coming kingdom. God has first loved us (cf 1
Jn 4:10). This is why the news of the nearness
of the kingdom of God and the apostolic
kerygma of the death and resurrection of
Jesus Christ is good news. Only God accepts
us as we are without being scandalized. This
nucleus is at the heart of Christianity. It is
what is strongly emphasized in the Neo-

Catechumenal communities. Jesus was a grace as abundantly irritating to the Pharisees as he was a comfort for those shut out from society. Drunkards, drug addicts, murderers, prostitutes *can* find the hope for regeneration in the Church without the finger being pointed at them.

On hearing this announcement, if we want to be given that life which resists all the threats of death, namely eternal life, we are invited to believe. 'What must we do, brothers?' And Peter tells them: 'Repent and everyone of you be baptized in the name of Jesus Christ for the forgiveness of your sins' (Ac 2:37-38).

The proclamation of the Resurrection opens the Neo-Catechumenal Way. From it there begins the formation of community and the rebuilding of the Church. In today's pastoral situation the need for an initiation into a personal experience of faith is readily recognized.[2]

We lack vigorous faith more than information about religion: today almost everyone 'knows' that they have received his power of salvation. The principal weakness of Christians faced with a world in an advanced state of secularization and so strongly imbued with atheism is the lack of such a personal encounter. The kerygma of Jesus Christ, conqueror of death, not only forms the starting-point of the community; it is its permanent basis; it is constantly recalled that Jesus is the cornerstone and that 'there is no other name given to man under heaven by which we can be saved' (Ac 4:12).

WAY OF FAITH AND CONVERSION

Those who welcome the kerygma set out together, like a people, on a journey. It is a way of faith and conversion during which they learn personally what it is to believe. Faith is a journey. Abraham and Mary are the relevant paradigms. Abraham is the father of believers (cf Rm 4), the model of those justified by faith. Abraham was promised a son and a land. And God did indeed give him, in his old age, a son through his wife Sara who was barren. When God asked Abraham for Isaac, his beloved and only son (cf Gn 22:2), he obeyed and on the mountain God 'provided' a ram. The patriarch saw that God was faithful in his history, he learned to believe existentially. Leaning on God one receives the fruit of his promise (cf Heb 11:8-9). Mary undertook a way of faith.[3] She received a good news and believed it. She conceived, carried in her womb and gave birth to the Son of the Most High. Such a fruitful progression is to be repeated in the Christian. A 'new man' will be born by the power of the Holy Spirit if the word is believed, kept in the heart and safeguarded in life. For Christians Mary is not only the model of the fecundity of virginal faith but also an image of the Church. The catechumen will be carried in the womb of the Church until the moment of birth from the baptismal font. The greatness of Mary lies in her faith. 'Blessed is she who believed that the promise made her by the Lord would be fulfilled' (Lk 1:45).

This way – the disciples of Jesus were called 'followers of the way' (Ac 9:2) – is an authentic Catechumenate (a word often misused today), that is to say it is an initiation to the faith, to conversion and to baptism. As we are dealing with a post-baptismal Catechumenate it is called a 'Neo-Catechumenate'.[4] Over the course of a number of years the neo-catechumens discover the riches of baptism, hidden and hardly tasted. Down through stages, passages and scrutinies, and only with conversion, one makes a descent into the waters of death from which emerges a new man created by the Spirit of God. Etymologically 'to baptize' means to 'submerge in water' (cf Rm 6:3). This symbolism marks out conversion as an interior 'descent'.

If we recall the layout of the early baptisteries, going down the steps is the symbol of conversion, of a *kenosis*, of a descent into our true reality. Going down we discover the truth about ourselves. Humility, says St

Teresa, is to walk in the truth.[5] Gradually the masks behind which we hide and defend ourselves fall away. At the start none of us recognizes ourselves concretely as sinners, no one has enemies; we all have bags of faith and are very loving. But through seeing ourselves in the mirror of the community everyone begins to discover the need to ask the Church for faith which rightly takes place at the first scrutiny. Before beginning to construct one has to do the demolition.

In the measure to which the Word of God enlightens us three fundamental truths are learnt along the way. The first and most essential is that Yahweh, the Father of our Lord Jesus Christ, is *the only God*, and that to love him with all one's heart is to have life (cf Dt 6:4-9; Lk 10:25-28). To sing the *Shema* is to call to mind the oneness of God, practically and not simply theoretically. In front of the one God, money, work, human loves stand revealed in their incapacity to save us and in their tendency to be transformed into idols. Turning to God takes place at the centre of our life, starting with the realities which capture our hearts. Christian conversion is much more than the renunciation of what is easily objectified and quantified. We have to be tested with the same temptations to which Jesus was subjected (cf Mt 4:1-11 and parallels). The Tempter provokes us into securing our life through money, rejecting our history, and bowing down before idols. These temptations, which certainly accompanied Jesus in his public life, redactionally placed by the evangelists at the beginning of his preaching, are temptations which are close to us today. They all aspire to the unique place owed only to God. Like the people in the desert we want bread this minute, here and now, without any dependency upon God. We try to insure our lives with money instead of trusting in the providence of our heavenly Father. Jesus was tempted in his own history. If he was to throw himself from the pinnacle of the temple and the angels were to support him then everyone, seeing the miracle, would be bound to recognize him as the Messiah. Where does Jesus, an unknown rabbi coming from the backwater of Nazareth, think he is heading? What can he hope to achieve with that band of disciples who can hardly make sense of him? Is this what is meant by 'the approaching kingdom of God'?[6] We are all tempted in our history. Can God really have loved us in making us be born in that place, with those parents, and these limitations? Finally it is not only Israel which makes its idol of gold. We are all tempted by the idolatry of power, to be subject to its dynamism, to lie down before the 'cause' –

which has so many names – and to grovel at the feet of others. Only acknowledging Yahweh as the one God gives true liberty (cf Jn 8:33-36). Israel falls into the temptation, while Jesus stays totally faithful and opens the way of fidelity. Psychology and sociology show how deep are the roots which bind us through property, power, knowledge, affection, and self-aggrandizement. To throw light on such depths in a way that gives life is really to free us.

The catechumens will need to give powerful signs that money is not their god. They will learn, for example, to love their children without wanting them in their own image and likeness, to love them starting from the fact that God has made them free persons. During the way catechumens discover the hidden traumas of their past history and learn to be reconciled with it. It is a question of passing from the false conviction that this and that has happened because God does not love us to the recognition that God loves us and saves us in our history. It is of prime magnitude to discover that the cross is a sign of the love of God and not the expression of his animosity (cf Gn 3:5). Our suffering brings us to the real dimension of our lives and from fragility it is much easier to open up to God.

Catechumens are called to inherit a blessing, to 'talk well' of God when considering their own lives. When we make this discovery we have found a radical peace. All the history of salvation carried out by God with his people is paralleled in some mode in the particular history of every individual. This principle is also applied in reading and interpreting the Scripture. The power of God comes to exorcise all the realities on which we rely in an idolatrous fashion. Conversion consists in making the transition from idols from which we ask for life to creations for which we bless God as we use them. It is important to guard against any overwhelming pessimism for God's creations are good (cf Gn 1). But our sin reduces them to the state of idols and this is why they must be rescued by the dynamism of redemption.

The second scrutiny is a probing confrontation with the temptations of money, our life story and our idols. It is a decisive stage in the Neo-Catechumenal Way. One's freedom with regard to money needs to be very clearly shown, as self-deception in this matter is particularly subtle, and relapses obstinate and recurrent. Renunciation of money leaves us free to be faithful to God. It is a tangible proof of trust in the God who is providence. It is the interpretative point through which to understand Christianity.[7] It is the basis for universal human fraternity as resplendently brought out in Francis of Assisi. Renunciation of economic, political and ideological and other interests is the quality of that 'poverty of spirit' which opens the way to truth.

During the process of conversion the second discovery, to be made without self-justification, masochism and exasperation, is of *sin*. It is a centrally important discovery which places us in the depths of our reality and enables us to see that only God is good; the glory belongs only to him. From it comes the heart by which we understand and do not judge our brother. A drunkard does not accuse another drunkard. God loves us because we are poor sinners. His freely given pardon both makes possible and requires the forgiveness of the enemy. 'As the Lord has forgiven you, forgive others too' (Col 3:13). An awareness of sin radically purifies the heart. It leads to a penetrating discernment of the evasions and rationalizations which deform us.

The third discovery is that of the *glorious cross*. God has changed the ignominious death on the cross into a reason for hope, glory and salvation through raising Jesus. The cross no longer destroys us if we are united in faith to Jesus Christ. The cross is the mystery of the wisdom of God (cf 1 Cor 2:7). It is the key for decoding the universe. Catechumens learn to look upon the cross as a meeting with God. The foolishness of the cross confounds the wisdom of the world. Its weakness conquers the power of the proud. God showed his providence in the cross of Jesus so that our 'deaths' do not kill us. In the mystery of the cross 'truth and life are united'.[8] Truth is revealed in the word of God for those who listen, for the catechumens. Life is offered by the Spirit who raised Jesus from the dead. 'Death' is everything, at work, in illness, family life and so forth, that we would prefer to be rid of immediately. However everything which has the appearance of death has been overcome in Jesus Christ. Those who listened to the initial catechesis and begin the Way in community with the first scrutiny are led to this discovery. The scrutiny takes them into the Catechumenate proper, putting in front of them the glorious cross with which they are signed.

Jesus is the Servant of God who, in the words of the famous songs of Isaiah, is 'sustained' by God. He has received 'the tongue of a disciple'. Yet he does not have 'a human appearance' for he is 'laden with the sins of the world' (cf Is 42:1-9; 49:1-6; 50:4-11; 52:13-53). The Servant of Yahweh is our unique truth. He is a sign of contradiction; for many a scandal, for others a force of salvation (cf 1

Cor 1:23-24). In terms of exegetics E. Kase-
mann has shown how all the Pauline formulae which speak of the benefit of Christ's
death for us refer back to the words of the
Last Supper. These in their turn are con-
nected with the fourth hymn of the Servant of
Yahweh. From the beginning the baptismal
catechesis introduces the Servant (cf 1 Pt
2:21-25).[9] The Servant of God is a constitutive discourse for Christianity but one that
needs careful handling. R. Bultmann recognized that the place, if anywhere, to meet the
originality of Jesus is undoubtedly in texts
such as these: 'You have heard how it was
said: An eye for an eye, a tooth for a tooth;
but I say to you: Do not resist evil. On the
contrary, if anyone hits you on the right
cheek, offer him the other as well' (Mt 5:38-
9). Or 'Love your enemies and pray for your
persecutors' (Mt 5:44).[10] To pass over these
mysterious words in silence would be a
betrayal of Christianity. But they are scandal-
ous and difficult. Obviously they are not to
be put at the service of ideologies of submis-
sion. They have to be put into the context of
the concrete manner in which Christ took on
the condition of a Servant: his words and
gestures do not show the weakness to which
F. Nietzsche refers. Yet as he died he forgave
and referred the judgement to God. The
cross and the Servant of Yahweh are both

revelations 'in the mystery'. They never lose their hidden character. They are not like an enigma which disappears once it is resolved. But blessed is he who has 'understood' the 'mystery' of the cross!

It is now a well established fact that, as part of the process of faith and conversion to baptism in the Neo-Catechumenal community, the sacrament of conversion, of penance, is powerfully restored. The witness of presbyters is that the communities have decisively strengthened the celebration of the sacrament in their parishes, sometimes even rescuing it from oblivion or from being pointless. This is understandable in theological terms. Baptism, from the beginning, was the great sacrament of conversion; reconciliation a 'second baptism', a 'raft of salvation after the shipwreck'. Penance was then grafted into a process of conversion within a community. The connotations with baptism, ongoing conversion in the face of the mercy of God shown in his Word, its ecclesial character, are irreplaceable aspects in the celebration of forgiveness. During the Neo-Catechumenal Way one discovers with clarity that sin pays the sinner with death, and at the same time experiences the communal character of sin and reconciliation. The first penitential celebration is prepared for with a catechesis of great theological concentration and significance. Through that celebration the participants joyously discover that they have received forgiveness alongside others in the Church. Receiving forgiveness frees us to be able to communicate with the others and happily and festively share food.

Other fundamental realities are integrated into this faith and conversion process. If one has begun to find life and find one's history enlightened through the proclamation of the death and resurrection of Jesus, then he will gradually be recognised with gratitude as *Kyrios*, the one to which everything is subject. One moves on from the soteriological dimension to a meeting with the person of Jesus Christ: in the power of the Risen One we recognize his divinity. This catechetical process is linked to the development of the Christological discussions in the early Church. It is highly relevant in our times when we need to rebuild the Christian identity in personal terms from its foundations.

The same process takes place with regard to *Eternal Life*. If the catechumens are now living a life which transcends death in the sense that they love the enemy and are not running away from their history, then this is a Life which is eternal. It is an experience which strengthens the hope of Life in its fullness beyond this world. Once entered upon, this Life is a guarantee of the fulfilment of the hoped for promise. See how theology understands the interpretation of the eschatological formulae.[11] The full realization is anticipated in the salvation which has already been received. Eschatology is the horizon of Christianity where horizon means not only the skyline that always stays in front of us but the whole environment within which we walk. Within this eschatological dimension we also discover the reality of judgement and hell. The good news of Jesus implies a judgement as to salvation or ruin. The gift we have received is measured by the abyss that would come with its loss. A Christianity where eschatology, both as embarked upon and as fulfilled, fails to carry out the task it so clearly played in the primitive Church is crippled and superficial. Rest is waiting for the pilgrim people, while for non-believers there is the risk of final perdition. Surveys of the contemporary religious situation show a discrepancy between an acceptance of the existence of God and of the hope after death. Many accept that there is a God while denying the 'beyond'. This raises a question mark for the Church and points out an area of Christian initiation that cannot be avoided.

The same process of faith and conversion also reveals the Father of our Lord Jesus Christ. If in Jesus we have known God's work for us, then we are led by the Spirit of Jesus to call upon him as our *Abba*. The atheist and the secularized can also enter into Christian faith. The Way does not presuppose faith. It is a way to receive it. Later on the Church will hand the symbol of faith on to the catechumens. And the catechumens will hand it back professing it publicly on the testimony of their own lives.

This process of faith, in the divinity of Jesus, in eternal Life, in God as Father, becomes real in the lives of the members of the community – for some with a surprising radicalness, given that they started from close to zero. At the beginning nothing is asked of those who start the Way other than that they listen with an open heart to the Word of God. This Word is like the seed of faith, of a new creature (cf 1 Pt 1:23). In the measure in which we are renewed by the Spirit (cf Gn 3:1f). we will be able to testify and to do the works of the new life. The working of the Spirit of Jesus shows itself in a love with the shape and dimension of the cross.

THE COMMUNITY AS REALIZATION OF THE CHURCH

The kerygmatically based preaching leads into the formation of community in which, as in the womb of a mother, the catechumens can be carried to faith. The preaching is not a series of talks without a follow-up but the starting point for a community process. The Neo-Catechumenal community is not an informal group. It is not a 'base community', a catholic association, a spiritual movement nor an elite group within the parish.

The Neo-Catechumenal community is the Church of Jesus Christ as realized in a particular place. There, where the Word of God is proclaimed, where the sacraments of the Kingdom are celebrated – whose 'concentrated expression' is the risen Jesus – where in a concrete way people meet as sons of the same Father and as 'drawn close together' in Jesus Christ, there the only Church of God, holy, catholic and apostolic, is made present, realized and manifested. In this sense a 'local Church' can be the cathedral of the bishop, the parish church presided over by a parish priest, or the smallest Christian community presided over by a priest in communion with his bishop (cf *Lumen Gentium*, 26; *Sacrosanctum Concilium*, 41-42). One of the most far reaching innovations of the Second Vatican Council is to have put into relief the local community which believes, celebrates the Eucharist and lives in fraternity and in this concrete way is a sign for all people.[12] The Neo-Catechumenal community is a local realization of the *infra* and *intra* parish Church. The ecclesiality which constitutes the Christian condition passes through the community which grows up within the parish in communion with the diocesan bishop. On this point the outlook of the Council is clearly visible. The Neo-Catechumenal Way as community, which is what it is in the Church, would be clearly unthinkable without Vatican II.

The community is always presided over by a presbyter. It is set within the parish. And the catechists, in order to open the Neo-Catechumenal Way in a diocese, receive the assignment from the bishop. He both welcomes and sends them. The relation of the catechists with the bishop and the parish priest are always above board. There is not the least ambiguity in this matter of ecclesial communion. There is not a twofold hierarchy in the community : one which comes down from Kiko passing through the catechists of the community and reaching the 'responsible'; and another which comes from the bishop and through the parish priest eventually reaches to the presbyter of any other community there may be in the parish. The Neo-Catechumenal Way is God's instrument for the rebuilding of the Church here and now.[13] The catechists are sent by the bishop and work in communion with the parish priest. Where they open the Way they take on the responsibility for carrying it through to its conclusion. When the catechumens renew their baptismal promises the catechists have carried out their task and present these adult Christians to the bishop. If any conflict should arise the catechists ask only that if the Neo-Catechumenal Way is to continue it be without adulteration. If the attitude of the parish priest makes this impossible, the catechists will withdraw completely from the parish. It would be absurd for them to exert any kind of pressure or to scheme behind the parish priest's back; likewise for the parish priest to use the group created in the parish to direct them according to his personal views, however legitimate these may be in their own terms, when these are different from those for which he invited the catechists and which were the basis on which the group of people came together. Obviously conflicts are not impossible but reciprocal communication can resolve them, and in the last instance the bishop has the final word.

The Church which is being constructed in the community is the 'visible body of the risen Christ'. It becomes the sign that the power of Jesus Christ, victorious over death, destroys the barriers between people and creates *koinonia*, or 'communion'. 'If we love one other it is because he rose from death,' says one the early songs of the Neo-Catechumenal Way. 'We know that we have passed from death to life because we love the brothers' (1 Jn 3:14). The Church is the 'body', the social presence, where the world is shown that death is overcome by those who believe in the God who raised Jesus from the dead and allow themselves to be led by the Spirit of the One who has risen. The Church is the visible proof that faith takes flesh and that the promise of God is historically accredited.

The Church is, at the same time, an assembled community and a reality professed in the symbol of faith in unity with the Spirit. We believe in the Holy Spirit who inhabits, sustains, and acts in the Church. The Church is the *locus* for the presence and action of Jesus Christ through his Spirit. The Church as 'sacrament of salvation' is constituted by the indissoluble unity between 'being community' and 'means of salvation'. Little by little the catechumens discover the two perspectives. One of the more surprising discoveries is that after some time has been spent in the Way, Christians begin to see themselves as 'part of a whole', as members of a community. They come to experience powerfully that there is no possibility of being Christian without the Church, which they meet concretely in the community. They begin to see the community as their own competence. The Church gradually begins to grow within their spirit breaking down religious individualism. They move from considering the Church as an organization for religious services, to live it as a community of brothers and sisters for whom they should be concerned. They are the *domestici fidei* of whom St Paul speaks (cf Gal 5:10). Besides living this growth in faith and conversion alongside each other, they discover the nurturing power of the Church. In the community the Church begins to be understood as a mother who brings them to faith. Within the Church which they begin to love they have received the Spirit of Jesus Christ who is re-making them from within. The picture of the Church as a large, empty structure – as might have been harboured in bygone days – is finished with. They begin, instead, to love her in her past history. They feel they are in the same boat and co-responsible for her future. This discovery of the Church, which was one of the fundamental contents of the primitive Catechumenate, is an undoubtedly fruitful recovery.[14]

Those who welcome the preaching of the kerygma into their lives enter the community and want to start a way of faith and conversion. There are no other conditions. Men and women, old and young, married and unmarried, educated and illiterate, rich and poor, priests and sisters can be in a community. No-one is privileged (cf Gal 3:27-29; Col 3:11). We are not talking about a group of those who besides wanting to deepen their faith belong to the same social background, or have the same lifestyle or whatever. From a sociological point of view the community is a 'mirror image' of the world and the differentiated 'body' of Jesus Christ. The fact that all the barriers of age, sex, culture, money and so on are dismantled and communion is born is itself a sign of the power of Jesus Christ. For this reason it is a call and a leaven for a wounded and divided world. It is a good thing that early on the different ideals of community, which we all have, begin to tumble down. Such projections of community are more often based on our dreams than on the action which God wants to bring about.[15] From the beginning of the Neo-

Catechumenal Way young people have been numerous. In general terms the communities have taken more in urban rather than rural areas. Perhaps the anonymity of the town makes us freer, or the experience of the crowd creates the need for a more personal space. In some countries there are communities which include Anglicans and Protestants. There are communities of pagans. Many members, who on their own testimony were looking for something, claim to have found what satisfies their spirit.

The community, the Church of Jesus Christ in a particular place, thanks to its sacramental character can be salt, light and leaven (cf Mt 5:13ff; *Lumen Gentium,* 9). In it the power of the risen Lord is reflected and active. The Church exists out of the love God has for all men. The Church saves the world by showing love towards the enemy as made possible by the Spirit of Jesus. Love and unity are the signs through which the Church witnesses to Jesus Christ and through which every human being can recognize him : love in the way that Jesus loved us, namely in the dimension of the cross (cf Jn 13:34-35) and unity between those who formerly were scattered by sin (cf Jn 17:21). These signs can be recognized by everyone, including those who have no faith, the far-away. Centrally the proper significance of this Way within the Church is to show the love of God for the lapsed. They are not open to any sign from God other than that of a new quality of relationship between people which they see with their own eyes. The witness of some on their own is insufficient. What is required is an ecclesial manifestation. The Neo-Catechumenal Way is therefore a way of evangelization in our secularized, de-Christianized and unbelieving world. Only the sign of an evident harmony of life and faith will be attractive and inviting today. In this sense it is very clear to the Neo-Catechumenal communities that the Church has an 'inside' and an 'outside'. A Christianity which is just based on customary habits is clearly insufficient; and it makes no sense to talk of anonymous Christians. To say this does not mean that only those who become part of the Church are saved. God is close to everyone and mysteriously accompanies everyone on their journey. The Church is sent with the power of the One who has risen to all the world as a seed and sign of the Kingdom of God (cf Mt 28:19). But the Lord has left no word as to how many will become his disciples. The Church is already saving the world. She shows love to the enemy. She takes upon herself the sins of those who reject her. In her womb she gives joy to the hapless. By her priestly character she intercedes on behalf of the world and makes her own the mission of the Servant of Yahweh.

The health of the Church can be particularly measured by the apostolic impulse. A Church which is timid or has pretentions is a sick Church. The apostles know that God has labelled the last place as theirs (cf 2 Cor 4:7-12); that they carry in their bodies the death of Jesus; that the Lord goes before them in their mission; that the joy that comes from being rejected for the Gospel is a real one (cf Mt 5:11-12); that the Spirit speaks through those who are sent. The apostolic drive of the Neo-Catechumenate is admirable. In 1968 it reached Rome and from there has since spread throughout the world. This diffusion has been carried out through the 'itinerant catechists' who go out from their respective communities to attend to the requests that have been made. Periodically they return to their communities by whom they continue to be supported. There are three marks which characterize the apostle in the conviction of the Neo-Catechumenate. They have to be sent by the Church in the person of those who preside over the Church. They are witnesses to the Resurrection on the basis of a personal meeting with the living Lord. And finally they go unprovided for in terms of money and security. In the summer of 1984 a thousand itinerants had the experience of their own mission in being sent all over the world. Listening to their accounts of this experience it was difficult not to imagine that a similar historical occasion had to be at the basis of accounts such as that in Matthew 10. Evangelization takes place to bring people to faith and conversion and to help in the reconstruction of the Church in our generation through the way opened by God. It is not a pretext for expanding membership. It is to proclaim the death and resurrection of Jesus Christ as the free gift of salvation for the poor of the earth. Given that these itinerants know at first hand that the Neo-Catechumenal Way is a concrete way to evangelize, when the door is not opened in one place they go on to another.

The community is the context in which the Word of God resounds and acts with power. The Scriptures take flesh when proclaimed within the Church to whom, as the bride of Christ, faith is guaranteed and for whom understanding is promised through the anointing of the Holy Spirit. According to the theologically well grounded presentation which is made in the Neo-Catechumenal Way, the Word of God, the Scriptures and the Church form an indestructible unity. The origin of the Church, which becomes the lasting foundation of every Christian community, is in the event of Jesus Christ alive and risen who today continues to call to faith and conversion. When Christ appears, victorious over death, he calls his disciples together again and this properly is the birth of the Church. The disciples, strengthened by the power of the Holy Spirit, are sent by Jesus to be his witnesses bringing a word of salvation (cf Ac 1:8) to the ends of the earth. Those who believe in the apostolic message receive the Holy Spirit. They are gathered together into a community which pre-dates them, in the middle of which lives Jesus Christ. The preaching of the Word is an event. It has power and is the seed of a new creation (cf 1 Pt 1:23-25). The Word of God is like the rain which descends on the earth to make it fruitful (cf Is 55:10-11). In itself it has the power to save those who welcome it and judge those who reject it. The Church, therefore, is born not from a book but from a Word laden with the power of the Holy Spirit.

The writings were preceded by the life of the Christian community in its missionary, catechetical, liturgical and ethical activity. The Scriptures are the sedimentation both of the proclaimed Word and the life of the Church. The Word goes before, accompanies and goes further on than the Scriptures. The event of the living Jesus Christ cannot adequately be enclosed in writings. Through the Holy Spirit, the giver of life to the Church, the Word of God creates new men. So the Scriptures are a dead letter without the Church, without a community which witnesses to what they announce. In the Christian life the Scriptures take on life and in turn Christians understand that their own history is contained within the Scriptures. For this reason one who scrutinizes the Scriptures always hears the Word of God in Jesus Christ and meets this same living Jesus Christ (cf Jn 5:39). And at the same time Christians find a Word directly personal to them. The risen Jesus is the fulfilment of the Scriptures which, in turn, are made real in the Church. This is why a Christian assembly which proclaims the Scriptures is much more than a book. It is the ambit whithin which the text is soaked with life by the Holy Spirit.[16]

The catechumens are brought to faith within the community. The community is much more than the sum of the members who form it, as can effectively be seen from the fact that each individual member receives more than could be given by all the others. The Word to which they listen and which has set them in motion becomes an insistent call. It is a mirror of the interior power which animates the community. It is a reality understood in a more living way in the 'resonances' of the brothers and sisters. Perhaps many of the forms of service to the

Word (such as retreats, cursillos, conferences) have remained without fruit because
there has not been a community in which
one hears the 'echo' of the word as something continually offered to everybody. The
community is the primordial place in which
the Word of God becomes real. Its proclamation is looking for a welcome, and it is difficult for it not to have been heard by someone. Is this not how 'Word of God' and
'Church' come to be inseparable in the hearts
of catechumens? Given such a rich context of
Word, Scripture and Church one can see why
those entering the Catechumenate ask the
Church for such a personal reality as faith.
The Christian is born into the Church. The
experience of community as a living environment, as the place where the Word of
God is actualized, as a space for the spirit of
faith and conversion, is a primordial experience of the Catechumenate. One completely
fails to understand the originality and richness of this Way if one does not go down
deeply enough to reach these Christian realities and to the personal harmony which
each member increasingly recognizes. Otherwise we remain at the more or less phe-
nomenological level of what is a community
and how it works. We would generalize in
such a way as to bracket in the same framework communities or families of communi-

ties which are significantly different. An adequate judgement needs to bear in mind not only the psychological and sociological aspects, and how the community works in ecclesiastical terms. But more important are the further questions as to what Christology, what image of man, what concept of Christian mission sustain a specified community.[17]

To the extent that individual Christians allow themselves to be re-created by the Word of God different ministries and charisms begin to appear within the community. The Church as the body of the risen Christ has many members and in each one of them the Spirit is manifested for the common good: priests, deacons, 'responsibles', catechists, cantors, readers, *ostiarii*, widows, virgins, married couples and so on. The shared Christian vocation reverberates in many different ways in its members. Some ministries and charisms which have already been bestowed come to be rediscovered while others are found for the first time as personal callings. The presbyter learns to re-orient himself within a community which is eminently active. Alongside the others he is on a way of faith and conversion, but for the others he represents Christ as Head and Shepherd. Married couples discover the Christian greatness of conjugal love and the dignity, which comes from God, of collaborating in the handing on of human life. Their family is called to conversion in a 'domestic Church'. The 'responsible' does not have the same position as the priest in the running of the community. In one of its aspects his mission is that of being a link with the catechists of the community in order to ensure faithfulness to the Way. In another it is to take care of the organizational details and workings of the community. Some discover a vocation to the ministry of the presbyterate. They begin to study theology in union with the bishop and his seminary. Others find that they are called to the religious life. Others discover particular forms of lay apostolates because in addition to the common participation of all the laity in the salvific mission of the Church, there are specific ways, as an individual or in an association, of carrying out the mission requested by God.[18]

The lay apostolate cannot just be identified with its forms of association, but on the other hand we can be forgetful of the need for such apostolic associations. So although in the post conciliar period the apostolic movements have not flourished, we should not conclude that there has been no lay apostolic activity, sometimes of splendid worth. The Neo-Catechumenal communities stay within the common apostolate inherent in being a Christian. For this reason as part of the catechumenal process there is a real initiation to evangelization. Missionary activity is constitutive of the Catechumenate. However such an initiative cannot be identified with specialized apostolates as carried out by the apostolic movements. Just as there are members who, little by little, discover the call to be presbyters or religious, so there are others who find a concrete vocation in belonging to specific forms of the lay apostolate, such as Caritas.

Let us conclude this section on the major basic intuitions which characterize the Neo-Catechumenal Way. *Kerygma, Way* and *Community* are the three dimensions which structure this initiative raised up by God in the Church to contribute to her renewal and the salvation of the world. The three dimensions are mutually interdependent. The proclamation of the kerygma opens a way of conversion and creates communion among those who welcome this Word of salvation. At the same time faith is received or developed in the community. In it one can complete the descent, the *kenosis* into our reality which is often unrecognized and rejected. There is no catechumenal dynamic without the Church. Through those sent out by the bishop, she carries the way forward.

II

DESCRIPTION OF THE NEO-CATECHUMENAL WAY

We have considered the major intuitions that nourish and sustain the Neo-Catechumenal Way. It is only by going to this level that one can understand its originality. It is highly relevant in theological terms and brings the fundamental Christian realities harmoniously together. It has its own particular emphases which within the communion of the Church are not only legitimate but have proved fruitful. The brief descriptions of the different steps of the way which now follow presuppose all that we have said so far.

THE WAY:
GRADUAL AND ARTICULATED

The Neo-Catechumenal Way is gradual,
even if this is pleonastic. It adapts to the
rhythm of conversion and to the vitality of
people's faith. It waits without demanding
and stimulates without forcing. Such gradu-
alness does not imply that the Gospel is
'graded'. It is rather a progressive initiation
into the richness and total exigencies of the
Gospel. The Good News is a whole, and
nobody is authorized to water it down, but
there is a pastoral need to present it peda-
gogically. The way is certainly long. The
point at issue is not how quickly one can
finish but to meet in a deep way with the
risen Jesus Christ. Pastors sometimes show a
degree of anxiety as it seems to go on inde-
finitely. This is understandable. However it
must be remembered that growth to maturity
in the faith, required of an adult Christian and
for apostolic work, is slow. The candidate for
the priestly ministry is asked to undergo a
good number of years of spiritual, theological and apostolic preparation. A nun has to
do a juniorate and a novitiate before being

fully incorporated in the work of her religious family. Is it then so strange that one requires a period of time for a Christian to reach maturity? At times, then, impatience shows little understanding of the seriousness of the Christian lay vocation.

It must be remembered too that people can begin the Way from many different starting points: unbelief, personal disaffection, a wordly anti-Christian spirit, a natural religion unable to resist the powerful secularization of their surroundings, a perfectionist moralism of a pharisaical nature, a faith intermixed with political ideology of one kind or another. In such situations it will take time for the Christian adult to be born: realistic but full of hope, humble but bold, fraternal and a 'mystic as well as a witness in the world. It is not necessary to finish the Catechumenate before a Christian can begin to work in the Church and the world. The process of initiation gives rise to a gradual involvement in the activities which are an integral part of that same initiation. Undoubtedly the stages will, in time, be simplified. The length of the Catechumenate can be reduced, activities be lightened and the preparations made easier. But beginnings are invariably slow and tentative. One opens up the way by walking. The important issues are whether the content is solid and substantial, whether there is an openness to reading the signs, to calls from inside or out, to the experiences and the criticisms.

The different stages, within a certain flexibility, are actually fixed. Their articulation is the product of a meeting between the Catechumenate of the primitive Church and the experience of the pioneer communities.[19] The first creative inspiration has found a body, even if the search is not yet finished. The meaning of each step can only be fully known at the end of the Catechumenate because there is no substitute for personal experience and because, for reasons of prudence, a sense of the 'arcane' is cultivated. This is not because of a neurosis about secrecy but out of respect for the Way itself, respect for the people at a particular stage and for those who are coming on after. An unintended consequence is that it is seen to help the cohesion of the community. Each human group and every ecclesial group has its own particular identity which comes from the concrete givens which have shaped it. A group would lose its sharpness and vigour if it were forced to abandon these particularities. Its configuration would cease to be distinctive. All these secondary considerations are understandable within the overall context of the Way. Here one can recognize whether the creative genius has opened a distinctive way with its own identity or has simply put together bits taken from here and there which have no living coherence.

The first communities have already finished the Way. In 1983 the members of the first community of the Canadian Martyrs in Rome renewed their baptismal promises during the Paschal Vigil.[20] The question that now springs to mind is, 'Where do they go, these Christians who, after a long Catechumenate, have rediscovered the richness and responsibilities of their baptism?' As a matter of principle they should go back into their parishes, into the local Church, inside of which they have been brought to maturity in the faith. Our parishes, however, are still tied to a previous image of the Church as the locus for the organization of religious services rather than the Church as community. This is why the new wine sometimes has a greater capacity for fermentation than the 'mother' into whose womb it is poured. We will have to wait for the parish to be renewed so that the Christians who finish the Neo-Catechumenal Way can be inserted into an already reinvigorated nucleus. In fact one begins to see this new reality in parishes where there are many communities.

The whole itinerary of the Neo-Catechumenate is supported by a *tripod* of Word, liturgy and communion. This tripod was discovered during the experience in the shanty town. It matches the constituent realities and vital actions of the Church as it is found in a particular place. The Word of God nourishes the faith. At the eucharistic table in blessing God we enter into the dynamism of the Jesus Christ dead and risen. In these ways the Church comes to birth as the body of the Lord. 'In the legitimate local meetings the faithful come together for the preaching of Christ's Gospel and the mystery of Lord's Supper is celebrated, "so that through the flesh and blood of the Lord all the members of the community may be united closely together"' (cf Ac 2:42).[21] The Word of God is proclaimed in communion with the bishops who are the successors of the apostles, the original witnesses to the Resurrection. The Eucharist is celebrated within this same communion. And so the local community is in a full sense the Church. The apostolic stamp in the three constitutive realities of the Church – Word, liturgy, communion – testifies to the ecclesiality of the community. Obviously, Word, liturgy and communion have the power to actualize the mystery of Jesus Christ because the Holy Spirit is present and working. In the shanty town it was found that the welcome given to the Word of God creates communion, and leads into a liturgy as a thankful joyous response. This discovery is carried forward into all the stages of the way. These are the means through which Christian initiation takes place. Experience has shown that a celebratory atmosphere creates a favourable climate for welcoming the Word of God.

All the communities celebrate the Word once a week. They meet on the Saturday evening for the Eucharist, to begin the Sunday rest. Communion is especially fostered by the monthly 'convivence'. Here everyone tells the others of their experience of their journey of faith. This is also the occasion for addressing any of the problems that might arise with regard to the journey of the community.

'Convivences' are an important aspect of the Neo-Catechumenal Way. Besides the frequent 'convivences' of a particular community there are others that begin the different steps of the Catechumenate. There are others, too, with the local catechists and the 'responsibles' of the communities which start the period of catechesis at the beginning of the year. And there are 'convivences' of Kiko and Carmen with the itinerant catechists. They are very important for maintaining the cohesion of the whole family of Neo-Catechumenal communities.

The two liturgical celebrations are prepared in turn by a 'team' of four or five people who present the various readings to the assembly through introductions. The celebrations are given special care with respect to the songs, lights, flowers, altar, ambo, presidential chair, and the meeting room... The liturgical signs are highly valued and one notices that they are of great efficacy in the community. Simplicity is not the enemy of beauty or dignity. After the Word has been proclaimed, but before the homily of the presbyter, the community is invited to talk with freedom of the 'echo' that the Word has produced in them. After the universal prayers the prayer of the faithful continues spontaneously. The celebration is slow and solemn, but keeps a celebratory rhythm.

The steps of the way are marked out by scrutinies, passages, exorcisms and rites which are not artificial constructions. The celebration which marks out a passage closes one stage and opens up another, and is eloquent because it brings together different elements. It is a *symbolic* celebration, one in which the signs speak in their own language. It is a celebration preceded by *catechesis* which has been given during a 'convivence' of some days' length and which explains the meaning and import of the signs. It is a celebration in which the *experiences of life* which have been touched by the catechesis and the march of the community are palpable. It is a celebration of the Christian assembly in which the Lord is present through his *Spirit*, according to his promise. So the celebration is not an empty one, thanks to the action of God in Jesus Christ through the Spirit. It is not arbitrary because the symbols speak to our deepest dimensions. It is not puzzling because the catechesis together with the Word of God illuminate where the signs are pointing. And it is not abstract because our existence is at stake. The celebrations do not stay at the periphery of the personal core of the believer. These passages vigorously point out God's promise for the next step and how we shall find ourselves in the next part of the track. God, with his Spirit, points out the horizon through which we, strengthened as we are, can walk in obedience. In the liturgy of the first scrutiny, for example, the rite of the signing with the cross is celebrated. Each person knows what his cross is, knows how the resurrection of Jesus has made it glorious and how, in consequence, we can embrace it with the certainty of finding it illuminated.

THE STEPS OF THEs WAY

a) The kerygmatic step

Everything begins when a parish priest expresses the wish to open the Neo-Catechumenal Way in his parish. At the Sunday Masses the parish priest will present a 'team' of catechists to his faithful. They talk, then, to everyone, inviting them to a catechesis for adults. The news of this catechesis is also made known throughout the parish by any other means available. This first step lasts about two months with twice-weekly catechesis. It has three parts.

The first helps those who are listening to grasp where they are. It culminates in the announcement of Jesus Christ conqueror over death and over what has the sign of death in our life. In a conclusive manner the resurrection of Jesus Christ is allied with the offer of a life of freedom for all those who believe and enter into conversion. The first part finishes with a penitential celebration whose ecclesial character has already been highlighted.

In the second part an initiation to the Word of God is begun, announcing the kerygma through the Scriptures. Abraham is a powerful word. He is the paradigm for belief and of how God provided when he called for the death of Isaac. 'It was by faith that Abraham when put to the test offered up Isaac. He was confident that God had the power to raise the dead; and so he was given back Isaac from the dead' (cf Heb 11:17.19). The Exodus from Egypt also shows the power of God to break the barriers of death. The people are freed from slavery to Pharaoh, pass through the sea into the 'great and terrible' desert, are fed and receive the gift of the promised land... So the power and topicality of this Word is insisted upon. 'Your chains can be broken now if you, too, call upon the Lord who has power over everything which keeps you enslaved.' So in this way the power of God, who raised Jesus from death and made him the way through death for all who believe, is testified to in the Scriptures. In the celebration of the Word, which is preceded by a catechesis on the relation of Word, Scripture and Church, the participants receive the Bible from the hands of the bishop.

Finally, in a weekend 'convivence', there is an initiation to the celebration of the Eucharist. First there is some catechesis and then a solemn, festive, and fully participatory celebration. This celebration has an unsuspected newness for everyone. The catechesis brings out the connection between the Christian Eucharist and the Jewish Passover. The Jewish background is highlighted throughout the Neo-Catechumenate not merely as a 'reference point' for understanding the origin of many Christian realities, but above all as an historico-salvific way which leads us to the fulness of Christ. In terms of the Eucharist the catechesis highlights the element of benediction and thanksgiving to a God who passes by to take us from death to life, slavery to freedom, fear to peace, from darkness to light and from sadness to joy. The Neo-Catechumenal Way is presented during the 'convivence' so that everyone might know what it is about. And the mission of the Church is expounded: the mission of the Servant of Yahweh. The Sermon on the Mount is, for the Christian, the mirror image of the new man. The community is formed from those who want to begin the Way, and the 'responsible' and 'co-responsibles' are elected. The parish priest is the presbyter of the first community in his parish. Everyone has their first surprise when they meet again for their next celebration, because they have secret misgivings about what they are witnessing. They imagine that the heat of the 'convivence' is what excited everybody, and that everything will cool down with time and distance. But here they are, beginning a Way whose continuity is a sign of its ability to hold them together and give them real food.

b) The Pre-Catechumenate

The Pre-Catechumens follow the Way by celebrating the Word of God which is prepared by 'teams' who use the themes of *The Dictionary of Biblical Theology*.[22] Gradually they are brought close to the Scriptures through the two inseparable access routes of acquaintance and their own experience of life. The Saturday Eucharist is that of the Sunday which is anticipated to introduce us into the rest of the Lord. The readings are those given by the Church in the Lectionary. At the beginning of the Way not everyone may fully appreciate the implications of this, namely, that it is the Church that sets the Pasch in front of us. The reactions of many of those who are put into contact with the Bible for the first time can easily be imagined. There are people who have learnt to read in order to draw near to the Scriptures. Slowly and patiently within the community people are given the key, by the Church, to understand and be nourished by this book which was formerly sealed to them. In this step of the Way they experience the joy of listening together. They begin to see, too, the rebuilding of those who have been destroyed. On the other hand those who have 'always been Christians' begin to see that they do not have the faith they thought they had, and those who have been most assiduous that they do not love as much as they imagined. The community is like an arena in which everyone's egoism, projects and personal whims clash together. It is a mirror in which to know oneself. In the face of such realities everyone's ideals of community are broken down. Everyone has his or her own list of complaints. Quickly people come up against two alternatives – either all this 'mess' is going to collapse or the community will have to be built by God. They become aware that they need a new heart capable of loving those who are irksome and overbearing so that their childish faith can come to maturity. The faith which was sown in them like a seed at baptism has not grown to adulthood.

This step which lasts about two years ends with a 'convivence'. This consists of relevant catechesis, meetings in small groups and personal reflections and ends with the first scrutiny in the setting of a celebration which begins that journey which will end with the renewal of the baptismal promises. As part of this celebration everybody who wants to continue signs their name in the bible of the community. They ask the Church for faith so that they can reach Eternal Life. They show their willingness to receive the Holy Spirit and are signed with the glorious cross of our Lord Jesus Christ. The Church, dwelling place of the Holy Spirit, welcomes those who make this step into her maternal care. She will guide them, under her protection, to the renewal of their baptism. The Catechumenate is not simply a matter of chronology, a period of time which can be arbitrarily lengthened or shortened. Moreover one is not merely repeating the same things. Its variety and richness is, according to the step, put forward for the assimilation of people immersed in history. Time is needed in order to discover what it is to believe; time to uncover the mystery of the Church; time to discover the truth of the Sermon on the Mount which can be realized through the Spirit; time to move from a life of egoism to a life of service; time to discover that money is not the 'lord' who really saves... These are the discoveries that need to be made with a certain assuredness during the period of Catechumenate because that is what it is for. Later, when the Catechumenate has been finished, these basic Christian attitudes will be deepened still further.

c) Passage to the Catechumenate

This is a step which is called that of humility; a time to descend into one's own reality, namely, a knowledge, recognition and acceptance of one's personal situation. It is much easier to seek to avenge or to protest about one's life than it is to recognize it. Obviously these attitudes are not mutually exclusive. Our reality is the result of the providence of God, of personal decisions, of historical conditioning and of social influences which are not always beneficial. God's providence is not on a par with the other factors, rather it embraces them and is realized through them. X. Zubir says that providence is transcendent in immanence. The Neo-Catechumenal Way is particularly alert to seeing the will of God in the happenings of daily life. It understands that God shows us his love in our present situation and in our past history. Nothing happens or has happened by chance. Theological realism is a healthy outlook so as not to run away from one's personal reality by accusing others, including God himself. A fundamental change is to be reconciled with God in our own personal history; to move from complaining about our history, like the people of Israel in the desert, to blessing God because everything he does is done well and eternal is his mercy. This is the only way in which we can be healed in order to take on the evil in our world. The depths of our personalities are made up of a confluence of 'divine necessity' (cf Mk 8:31; Lk 24:26,44), of the wages of past sins paid with 'death', of the constitutive conditions of human liberty, and of the social character of human living which means that we find ourselves with different social opportunities and standards of living. To have light thrown on this deep-seated side of our personality is conversion.

The *Shema*, the life-giving recognition of God's uniqueness, is the yardstick of a conversion focussed on our affections. During the celebration of the first scrutiny the president tells the candidate for the Catechumenate: 'If you want to have Eternal Life you shall love the Lord your God with all your heart, with all your mind, with all your strength and your neighbour as yourself' (cf Lk 10:27). So the candidate needs to show that only God is Lord through renouncing money in a significant way. We have here the kind of realism that refutes facile accusations of 'angelism'. Money is *the* rival of God in our lives (cf Mt 6:24). It is not difficult to analyze the atheistic impetus of this 'powerful horseman' who enslaves man and destroys human fraternity. Any process of Christian initiation which does not touch our relationship with money is superficial and in the end unrealistic. The 'passage to the Catechumenate' is centred on this point. It is recalled in that step of the Way called the 'convivence of the *Shema*'.

The Neo-Catechumenal communities are sometimes accused of 'angelism', of being abstract and simple-minded in the face of the ins and outs of our complex socio-political reality. However the Neo-Catechumenal Way is fully aware at every point of our misery and clearly addresses regeneration in a concrete way. More generally one can ask whether St Paul was being 'angelist' when he wrote what he wrote to Philemon? Is not the heart of slavery rooted out when slave and master live the unique Lordship of Jesus Christ as brothers within the same working community? Moreover is there not a contradiction between the 'realistic' declarations of certain Christian groups and their evident sterility?

The celebrations of the Word of God in this step of the journey of the Catechumenate, which lasts about a further two years, focus on the major events in the history of salvation. These are Abraham, Exodus, Desert, Covenant, Promised Land, Kingdom, Exile, Prophets, Creation, Messiah, Resurrection, Church and Parousia. The community is introduced to each theme over a period of four weeks. The aim is for the Word of God to become bread, not to develop biblical erudition. This non-educative intention can sometimes become somewhat controversial because of the weight of insistence on what is basic, namely, the meeting with Jesus Christ. But this is not the same as excluding the study of the Scriptures and the Tradition of the Church as such. The questions which are always put explicitly ask how this event relates to Jesus Christ and how it touches concretely their own lives. These Christological and existentialist readings of the Scriptures are a constant. This springs from the certainty that the Bible contains the Word of God which takes on life within the Church and in every Christian. There is trust that God in fact speaks here and now seeking out the welcome of faith. We too are destined to be recipients of the Word of God. We are called to leave room for it so that it may become flesh in us. Reading the Word is profoundly personal, ecclesial and authoritative, resting as it does on the ministry of the Church. This authoritative character is shown in the community in the homily of the presbyter, the preaching of the bishop and the documents of the Magisterium.

This step ends with the second scrutiny. Catechesis on the temptations of Jesus and of Israel illuminate a rite in which possessions are renounced, as the Gospel asks of the disciples, and a powerful sign is given that

life will be sought only in God. In the first
scrutiny that Spirit was conferred that enables us – through his gifts – to love God
above all and one's neighbour in the dimension of the cross. Now the issue is posed as to
whether those talents have been traded to
effect in the struggle against the power of
money. It is not easy for us to be freed from
the spell which money exercises. However,
the process of such detachment is a necessary traverse in Christian conversion. Money
can decisively halt the process of Christian
conversion, while its renunciation removes
the chains on an estimable freedom and
lordship. In this rite realities, the renunciation of idols and adherence to the Lord,
imprinted at baptism (cf 1 Th 1:9-10) become
current. The invocation of the Holy Spirit is
for an exorcism by which the catechumen is
freed to follow Jesus. In the second scrutiny
a collection of a surprising amount of possessions is made in an absolutely free way and
the money is given to the poor of the parish.
The truth of this renunciation, the apostolic
impulse, the joy in the precariousness which
trusts in God, are pre-eminent signs of the
Neo-Catechumenal Way.

d) Catechumenate

This step, which lasts a number of years, is
characterized by simplicity in one's relation-

ships with God and with other people. All our life becomes transparent and simple when the darkness of our heart is enlightened. Complication and violence are not the marks of conversion. A 'baby' is growing up during the Catechumenate; a new creature who is the fruit of faith and of the Spirit, who trusts in God, who is aware of weakness and stops judging others. A new creature who seeks and asks God for a heart which is not proud.

From the very beginning the Church has given four things to those who want to enter into her house. These are the symbols of the faith, the Our Father, the commandments of God which are summarized in the *Shema* and in loving one's neighbour as oneself, and the sacraments. So the Church also gives these things to the neo-catechumens who will have to give them back to her after they have identified themselves with these realities. In successive stages there will be an initiation to prayer, in the way Christ taught his disciples. There will be the handing on of the Apostolic Creed in which the preaching of the apostles is concentrated as a *symbolum*, a distinctive sign of the faith of the Christian. These stages of initiation take place in the step of which we are talking.

The celebrations of the Word revolve around biblical personages, such as Noah,

Abraham, Isaac, Jacob and Moses. For the catechumen this is another way to meet the Word of God, to go deeply into the Scriptures, and above all to find in them Jesus Christ as the risen Lord. The Scriptures give us the Word through concrete figures: Abraham is Faith, Jacob Election, Joseph Providence, Moses the Leader of his people.

The catechumens are initiated into daily prayer, which for them will be a powerful weapon against the attacks of the evil one (cf Eph 5:10f). Every day they need to put on the weapons of light to hold out in the fight with the enemies who want to separate them from faithfully following Jesus. The psalms and the book of the Liturgy of Hours are given to them. In groups, in a liturgy in the home, they scrutinize the psalms with the help of the notes, the parallel passages and the other cross references of the *Jerusalem Bible*. Together they look for the relation which every psalm has to Jesus Christ. Everyone then puts their own life in front of the psalm. In this way they become familiar with the psalms which become their own personal expressions of entreaty, thanksgiving, praise and anguish. The Church has without modifying them made the psalms her official prayer. Enriched by this Christological and personal approach, the initiates receive this awe-inspiring prayer from the Church. With the handing on of the psalms the catechumens begin to pray Lauds at dawn everyday; on Sunday they are joined by their children. Through simple catecheses they pass on the faith to them. In the parish they collaborate with the catecheses for first communion, confirmation, baptism, marriage and so on.

A year after handing on the psalms the Church gives the catechumens the *symbolum fidei*. This recalls the *traditio* and *redditio symboli* of the primitive Church. Every article of the Creed is studied, made one's own and celebrated in the community. Everyone is asked to say whether they believe in this article and why. Response to the kerygma is not exhausted by welcoming the Lord as Saviour. The content of the faith has to be made explicit and accepted. The *fides qua* – that disposition of faith on which we base our existence in God – is enlivened in its dynamism and becomes specific in the *fides quae*, in the content of the rule of faith.[23] In order to be a witness to the faith it is not enough to refer to the authority of the Church. It is also necessary that one personally verifies the occurrence of faith in one's own life. Only in this way can the Christian be a witness. Formerly he could speak only of what he had heard; now he begins to believe because 'he has seen' God in his history (cf Jb 42:5). Obviously the experience of a single person is not the measure of what the Creed declares. That comes from the faith of the Church who, generation after generation, has lived with Christ and was visited by him in the appearances after his resurrection. But without that clear, sincere and authentic reflection which makes for personal conviction the apostle cannot be born (cf 1 Cor 9:1).

The catechumens are now called upon to profess their faith. 'I tell you, if anyone openly declares himself for me in the presence of men, the Son of man will declare himself for him in the presence of God's angels. But the man who disowns me in the presence of men, will be disowned in the presence of God's angels' (cf Lk 12:8-9). They now go, sent out two by two, to visit the families of the parish, with the agreement of the parish priest who tells the faithful about this.

They go to them announcing peace in the name of the risen Jesus Christ. In this way they become part of the evangelizing mission of the Church. In this mission, which is undertaken with fear and without any human defences, they come to understand how God has kept the last place for the apostles, how there is an inexpressible joy in being rejected for the name of Jesus, how God opens the ears of those who listen, and how welcome is a glass of water given to those sent by Jesus. In this way, although on a small scale, they join in the public proclamation of the Gospel, no longer keeping to the sanctuary of conscience or to the limits of the community. And so they come to assimilate the dispositions of apostles, to which catechumens have also to be initiated.

In the context of the catechumenal confession of faith, St Augustine has left us a striking passage in which he records what Simplicianus had told him about the philosopher Victorinus. The latter had converted to Christianity in his heart, and had told this secret to Simplicianus, but had not found the courage to profess his faith openly before the *plebs sancta*. Finally, when he was no longer ashamed of the 'signs of humility to the Word', he resolutely said to Simplicianus: 'Let us go the church, I want to become a Christian.' And Victorinus made his public profession of faith, much to the joy of the Christian community and the admiration of all Rome.[24]

In fact it is hard to break the clandestine character of the faith. It presupposes that one has understood that the gift one has received turns into a task one has to perform. And that there is more value in appearing publicly clothed in the humility of the Word than to keep up a social appearance that shamefully hides one's Christian identity. It is only when one thinks about the timidity which presently suffocates the Church in Spain, and I sense in all the other countries of Western Europe, in a pluralist and non-confessional world, that one can begin fully to appreciate the initiation into public profession made in the Neo-Catechumenal Way.

At the end of this period of proclamation from house to house the brothers and sisters make the *redditio* of the Creed in the assembly of the parish, publicly confessing the faith. Each one proclaims whether, why and what are their grounds for believing in terms of their lived experience. Those who have given back their faith to the Church, and in whom the Church has recognized her faith, carry palms in the procession of Palm Sunday as a sign of witness to Christ which can result in martyrdom.

After a further year there will be a new and more intense initiation to prayer. This is the step in which they receive the 'Our Father' from the Church. The Lord's Prayer can be said on the basis of our baptism (*institutione formati*).[25] The inspiration of the Spirit within us gives us the hearts of children (cf Rm 8:14-17; Gal 4:6) who have been instructed by the teaching of Jesus, living in fraternity with him without losing the audacity to call God *Abba*. God, who at the beginning of the Way was either a meaningless word or a 'mighty hand', now starts being the Father who treats the catechumen as his son.

e) Election

The passage from the Catechumenate to the election takes place in a liturgy in which the catechumens write their names in the Book of Life. Only those who have shown their faithfulness to the covenant with God in Jesus Christ move on to become *electi* or *competentes*. The works of Eternal Life are the credentials of the new creature. The catechumens can rest in the will of God and express the *Shema* in their life without effort, as if they have received a gift. It is a time for praise and thanksgiving, because they are called to inherit a blessing (cf 1 P 3:9). They are called to be the sacrament of salvation in the middle of the world, exercising a priesthood of spiritual worship on the altar of their own history. They intercede for mankind, taking upon themselves the mission of the Servant of Yahweh. In loving their enemies they show the love God has for sinners and for the far-away. They are the mirror of what God can do to rebuild broken lives. Just as Jesus died for the world on the cross, so the world receives life through the life of Christian service. I am not in a position to say more about this step apart from what can be gleaned from descriptions of the Neo-Cate-chumenal Way and from the experiences of those who have travelled it.

f) Renewal of baptismal promises

This is the last passage and, for those who have renewed their baptismal promises, it leads into the step of the 'neophyte', who lives in paschaltide. The Easter Vigil lies at the heart of the Neo-Catechumenal Way. This is why one can understand the privation of a community who cannot celebrate it with the full richness of all its signs. The Neo-Catechumenal Way does not ask for a cel-ebration on behalf of the members of the communities. It insists rather that the cel-ebration take place with all the richness of the readings and signs envisaged in the ritual of the Church. Safeguarding this it becomes secondary as to whether the celebration is in the parish or among the communities. The Vigil is celebrated with great solemnity. During it the children are catechized on the meaning and grandeur of this night and on the more important signs. In this Vigil the children of couples from the communities of the parish are baptized. The rhythm of the community moves from Easter to Easter. And it is on this holy night that the 'elected' renew their baptism. They receive the incomparable dignity of Christians or, to put it better, they discover in a life-giving way a dignity that had been hidden. The celebration of the Easter Vigil in its fullness is not a luxury. It is the translation into rite of the pre-eminent position that the resurrection of Jesus occupies in Christianity, one which is powerfully recovered in the Neo-Catechumenate.

Those who have renewed their baptismal promises have come to the end of the Catechumenate, but have not arrived at perfection. After a long and serious Catechumenate one understands the fundamental importance of being 'illuminated' (cf Eph 5:14; Heb 6:4; 10:32) by baptism. But it is also necessary to be on guard against any belief that one is safe from temptation or a fall. During the long apprenticeship in what it is to believe it will have been verified many times that one cannot rely on one's own strength. One has to cast oneself in humility on the power and mercy of God. Christians are always walking towards the heavenly homeland fruits of which they have already received in advance. With the renewal of the baptismal promises the catechists have concluded the mandate for which they were called into the parish. The mission of the Neo-Catechumenal Way finishes here. We are, therefore, talking of a charism with a mission of a well defined length.

According to the witness of the brothers and sisters of the first community in Rome[26] to have renewed their baptismal promises, the various steps gradually gave them new horizons. They have discovered 'our blindness and the need to ask for faith; our idols which enslave rather than save; the uniqueness of God; the necessity for prayer; the kerygma as life for the world; the relation with God as Father; forgiveness of the enemy as proof that the Spirit lives in us; the Servant of Yahweh as the only truth which goes beyond logic and every human expectation'.[27]

What has been written about in the previous pages is not a beautiful dream but a reality, borne out to a greater or lesser extent in the lives of countless communities presently spread throughout the world. It is thought that there are already some 10,000. So in this way the Catechumenate of the Church has taken flesh in an original fashion as a Christian initiation for our time. It is undoubtedly a serious but fruitful experience. It stands up to theological inspection and in its turn puts theology under scrutiny. It obviously has its own emphases, but loyally offers itself to be examined by the Church while asking for a space within the ecclesial communion.

III
FINAL REFLECTIONS

In the first section we sought to set out the basic inspirations of the Neo-Catechumenate. The Way is based on the announcement of the resurrection of Jesus as an invitation to freedom in the midst of everything which bears down on us with the signs of death. It is a Catechumenate in the proper sense of the word. Christian communities in which the only Church of Jesus Christ is revealed and realized are formed through it. All the dimensions of ecclesiality implied by Christian living can flow through them, though clearly only in a real communion with the parish, the diocese and the universal Church. In the second section we described the steps and passages of the Neo-Catechumenate, outlining the characteristics of each different stage. They are periods of time marked out by a particular dimension of baptism which are gradually put forward for the discovery of catechumens. Given our overall purpose we have not felt it necessary to go into greater detail. The previous pages have, however, also sketched out the stronger emphases of the Way, and in consequence some of its half-lights. The first have been legitimated theologically, while ways of throwing light on the others have been put forward. The extraordinary value and importance of the Neo-Catechumenal Way means that it cannot be put 'politely' to one side; such an attitude betokens a lack of a sense of responsibility for the gifts of God. But at the same time, too, the Neo-Catechumenal Way needs to be attentive to the above mentioned lacunae so that they can be filled.

The Neo-Catechumenal communities are a *charism* which has already received notable recognition as a way of the Spirit for the Church in our day. In the shanty town, at the very beginning, when the novelty stood out that much more, the then Archbishop of Madrid, Casimiro Morcillo (+1971) undertook a detailed scrutiny of the emerging reality. He approved it even in the face of some objections and gave it decisive support. When Kiko and Carmen were first invited to Rome in 1968, Morcillo gave them a letter of recommendation for the Cardinal Vicar, Bishop Angelo Dell'Acqua (+1972). Pope John Paul VI and Pope John Paul II have given clear signs of esteem and encouragement.[28] In general critics of the Neo-Catechumenal Way accuse it of a certain Protestantism, or a certain lack of social involvement, or of the creation of a parallel Church. The evaluations of the pastoral authorities of the Church, however, make it unwise for anyone to doubt its unequivocal Catholic identity.

It is a charism alongside other charisms. All of them are centred on living and working together within the universal Church, within dioceses and, as they are, within parishes. There is no sense, therefore, in any charism claiming to be the only way of salvation or being gently put to one side and silenced. Ecclesial communion can waste away because it is dispersed and fragmented or because it is put on such a narrow basis that the charisms, to enter into play, have to be 'domesticated'. If this happens they lose their own originality and capacity to enrich. An overall pastoral strategy breeds suspicion when it does not leave space for the initiatives of apostolates born outside the diocese in question; and when possibilities for evangelization which seem to be fruitful elsewhere are excluded on the basis of viewpoints which are debatable even in terms of their ecclesiology. For a particular Church is catholic in its ongoing 'give and take' with other Churches. Similarly to argue that particular social conditions – whether of 'pluralism', inner or outer city estates, economic depression, or population ageing – are a sufficient reason for excluding ways found valuable by the universal Church, is to fail to recognize that the fundamental problem of every person is always and everywhere the same. It is to think that in our current situation the basic polarity is other than that between faith and unbelief.[29]

The Neo-Catechumenal communities are not an apostolic movement, which by definition are fitted for particular social environments, age groups or tasks. The latter are to be located, as has already been said above, among the special types of Christian lay participation in the mission of the Church. The former are focussed on the common apostolic responsibility. Participation in an apostolic movement presumes a specific lay calling, although frequently it may well be the route for discovering Christian faith. And it will bring together particular patterns of life and personal qualifications. It cannot be legitimate to opt for the communities without leaving room for specialized movements and vice versa. It is simply counterproductive to put the two – community and movement – into a competition with each other. How can it be doubted that the Church needs vigorous apostolic movements? But these cannot be promoted if the communities are ignored, or the communities neglect the *raison d'être* of the movements. It follows that a community cannot be utilized as if it were an apostolic movement. Nor can its efficacy be judged by the number of, say, trade unionists to which it gives rise. It is legitimate, of course, to hope that, as in fact happens, the communities will give rise to special vocations as priests, contemplatives, Christian activists at work, in Caritas, as teachers and among the marginalized.

Today the Church realizes the necessity for re-creating the Catechumenate for adults lost many centuries ago in the Western world. There are seminaries for the preparation of candidates for the presbyteral ministry. There are novitiates and juniorates for incorporating aspirants into a religious family. We have apostolic movements for the Christian education of apostolic activists. So there are opportunities for people to be introduced to specific aspects of Christian living. But where is the possibility of being initiated into faith, into the Christian life, and into the Church as the people of God? But is this not in fact the direction that the charism of the Neo-Catechumenal Way is taking? The individual vocations – marriage, virginity, ordained ministrie, evangelical witness – will appear in the bosom of the Christian community. Today the Church must re-open the Catechumenate to bring people to faith and conversion. The *Ordo Initiationis Christianae Adultorum*, promulgated in Rome on 6 January 1972 is a step in this direction.

The conviction that we now find ourselves in a new stage of evangelization, particularly as regards the urgency of a second evangelization of Europe, is realized on all sides. The contribution of Cardinal Daneels, the final speech of Cardinal Hume and the important intervention of John Paul II at the Sixth Symposium of the Conference of European Bishops (Rome, 7-11 October 1985) are unequivocable in this respect. We need to emphasize the centrality of the proclamation of the Good News without losing ourselves in details. We need to insist upon the importance of the kerygma, almost always discounted under the weight of the doctrinal. Otherwise we are led to speak to non-believers and atheists in a language which only stammers out the experience of the paschal mystery. What is called for is a new, almost foundational experience, of what it is to be Christian in our culture, a new and living encounter, a personal discovery of being carried in faith by God, of the liberating power of the Lord Jesus Christ, of the Church as mother and family, of the forgiveness of sins, of eternal life already begun in man's return to God, of the other as brother and sister... For this, as John Paul II said at the Symposium: 'We must return to the inspiration of the earliest apostolic model... Only with the pouring out of the Spirit does the work of evangelization begin. The gift of the Spirit is the first motor, the first spring, the first breath of authentic evangelization. Evangelization must begin, then, by invoking the Spirit and searching to find where the Spirit is blowing (cf Jn 3:8). Some signs of this breath are certainly present in today's Europe. To find, sustain and develop them one needs to leave time-bound routines behind and go to where life is beginning, where we can see that the fruits of life "according to the Spirit" (cf Rm 8) are produced'.[30]

But the Church can only evangelize, and evangelize in this precise historical moment, in the measure in which she herself permits the regeneration of her heart by the Gospel. 'In today's world the handing on of the faith and of the moral values deriving from the Gospel to the next generation is under threat; a new endeavour of evangelization and catechesis is needed. The evangelization of non-believers in fact presupposes the self-evangelization of the baptized...'[31] The Neo-Catechumenal Way is opening an adult Catechumenate within the Church. Moreover because of the powerful synthesis between faith and culture on which it is based, there is already in existence a way of evangelization in our secularized world.

The bishops, in particular, are called to scrutinize the charisms of the Spirit. At the beginning it may be that such charisms bring changes to the regular life of the Church, but the places where life springs up have need of special attention, care and love. The ideal of the Church is not the peace of the dead, but a vitality which overwhelms and conquers us. Ecclesial communion is not any old kind of harmony, but a concord which proclaims the Good News. And this touches upon another major theme of the Second Vatican Council, namely, reform of the Church in order to introduce modern man to the life giving power of the Gospel.

The bishop in the diocese and the parish priest in the parish are the organs for the communion of the different realities of the Church whether these exist or are to be promoted (obviously according to a hierarchical scale of values). In order to be the bond of unity, they need to display breadth of vision, clear-sightedness, generosity, patience, loyalty, and the ability to encourage and correct, granted the communion in plurality that the Church has clearly affirmed in Vatican II. When the formation of mutually exclusive groups – on the basis of age, pastoral preferences, clerical associations approved by the Church – weakens the unity of the presbyterate in a diocese, then everyone needs to profoundly review their attitudes and behaviour regarding communion. What is required is a penetrating, encompassing and mutually respectful communion rather than uniformity.

We must not fall into the temptation of consensual sterility, nor forget that besides the 'apostolic fraternity' there exists a fraternity between Christians and presbyter which is of powerful benefit to the latter. It is a fact that in the Neo-Catechumenal communities the solitude of the priest is broken and a real and profound communication is established.

The Neo-Catechumenal Way has identified with considerable sharpness that the depth of man's lack of salvation lies in the slavery brought about by the fear of death, the wages of sin. The reality of the situation in the Christian view of things is such that it is not something residual that will pass with the progressive 'socialization' of man. Similarly it has powerfully perceived that the kernel of the salvation brought by Jesus Christ is the forgiveness of sins, the capacity to love one's enemy, and the power to carry the sins of the world upon oneself given by the resurrection of Christ. Christian anthropology confirms that regeneration comes from receiving, through the power of the Spirit, the freely given love of God, the creator. We have already noted how Pauline themes are strongly emphasized in the Neo-

Catechumenal Way We also have to emphasize that peace, love, and mercy flow out from the heart as the fruits of the Spirit..., while the fruits of the flesh are discord, division and licentiousness (cf Gal 5:16f). Man makes his own world and either consigns it to vanity or rescues it from slavery (cf Rm 8:18f).

Moreover, given the social and cosmic aspects of our nature, there is an influence of society and the world upon the individual. External conditions are not matters of indifference to the personal nucleus of someone who has been redeemed by the light. A Christian without work can be illuminated about his problem of unemployment, but the personal disequilibrium which comes from this social situation has its influence on the life of faith. There is a relationship between the new man and social conditions which is not simply one way from the former to the latter, but in some measure goes two ways.

In the Second Vatican Council the Church discovered *two fields for her mission*. The first, essential and irreplaceable, is to preach the Gospel so that anyone who listens can enter into conversion and become part of the new people of God. But the Church is also called to the world in its secularity, to join with all men so that the dignity of man can be enhanced, peace guaranteed, justice be established for all men, and the poor defended.[32]

The evil that exists in the world always raises a question mark which is especially emphatic for anyone who believes in God as a good Father. Evil comes from human limitation, from one's conditioning, from the wrong use of freedom, from a deeply rooted egoism. This evil has a certain mysterious 'theological necessity'.[33] Certainly faced with this situation Christians are clearly called to a reconciliation with God in their personal histories, which are often far from pleasant, and to be burdened with the sin of the world following in the footsteps of the Servant of Yahweh. But they are also called, as capacities and contexts allow, to a transformative role which is both personal and social. God who is 'first cause' does not take away the responsibility of 'second causes'. The world is also a task entrusted by God to free people (cf Gn 1:27ff). The Christian as Christian is not excused from this task. The Father of Jesus Christ is the creator of everything. The redemption embraces the whole of reality.

Christian faith properly becomes public when one professes it openly, moving out from the silence of one's own privacy or out from the horizon of the community. But there is a public presence of the Church in society when it brings its viewpoint and collaboration to where the cause of humanity and the direction of society is in question. For this reason the Church cannot close in on itself or allow itself to be shut off in isolation. Peace, unemployment, education, work... are occasions for the Church to exercise her public character. A body united to its pastors is required for such huge tasks. The Church cannot give in to the temptation to be enfeebled as a whole, while many vigorous points of unity are at work internally. Expressions such as the forgiveness of sins or love for the enemy call forth wry smiles when used in the arena of social affairs. This is also true when the major dimensions of Christian anthropology (as regards love, marriage, the right to life) are put in opposition to other conceptions of human life. In this way the accusation of 'angelism' can be extended to sectors of the Church who formerly applied it only to particular groups of the faithful. According to this dynamism the profession of the Christian faith and the service of mankind carries with it its own opprobrium (cf Heb 11:24-26), but also a liberating joy. Even though the Church is on occasion accused of a certain lack of respect for man because her invitation is to conversion and to faith, this call must not be quietened precisely out of concern for man's good as well as out of obedience to God.

What I have just finished saying is a call to the Neo-Catechumenal Way and to the whole Church. The requisite attitude to the Neo-Catechumenate is that towards a vigorous, fruitful charism which is called to keep alive within the Church certain clearly perceived profound emphases. The Church as a whole, as well as the initiators of the Way, have a duty before the Spirit of God, the source of all charisms, not to alter its nature. The fruitfulness of a charism stems from its originality. In order that the Church accept the charisms in their originality they must be discussed and sometimes the Church must protect them in their growth to maturity and in the clarification of their possibilities. It is therefore understandable that in the light of experience and of the needs of ecclesial communion certain revisions or adjustments will be called for. Such final touches and amplifications will have to be undertaken by the initiators of the charism and eventually by their legitimate heirs. To force change from the outside would be unjust and to risk altering the nature of the way. The health of the Church is shown in the generous welcome to initiatives raised up by the Spirit, and the truth of the charisms is accredited in their own availability to the ecclesial communion.

NOTES

[1] Cf Y. Congar, *Vraie et fausse Réforme dans l'Eglise*, 2 ed. (Paris, 1968).

[2] Cf K. Rahner, *Conversion* in *Sacramentum Mundi*, ii, section 3, (London, 1968) 6: 'In the age of atheism, which declares it cannot find in the question of God any meaning, even as a question, or discover any religious experience whatsoever, this spiritual art of conversion has not primarily a moral decision as its immediate goal, but the bringing about of a fundamental religious experience of the inescapable orientation of man towards the mystery which we call God.'

[3] Cf *Lumen Gentium*, 58: 'Thus, the blessed Virgin advanced in her pilgrimage of faith.' O. Semmelroth comments: 'Precisely in this faith filled with faithfulness Mary is converted into a type of the community of those who listen to the Word of God and keep it.' (*Kommentar zum VIII Kapitel* in H. Vorgrimler, ed., *Lexicon für Theologie und Kirche. Das Zwete Vatikanische Konzil. Documente und Kommentare* I, Freiburg i.B. 1966, col. 333). Also cf the Encyclical Letter *Redemptoris Mater: Mary in the life of the pilgrim Church*, Pope John Paul II, 1987.

[4] Cf *Notitiae* 85 (1973) 280.

[5] Cf *Interior Castle (The Mansions)*, VI, 10, 6, (London, 1974), 250-1; also *The Complete Works of St Teresa of Avila* (London, 1944).

[6] Cf G. Bornkamm, *Jesus of Nazareth* (London, 1973), 66-68; cf my book *Jesús, el Evangelio de Dios* (Madrid, 1985) 189 ff.

[7] Cf J. Sobrino, *Resurrección de la verdadera Iglesia; Los pobres, lugar teológico de la eclesiologia* (Santander, 1981) 109 ff; English translation: *The True Church and the Poor* (London, 1985).

[8] Cf L. Bouyer, *Christian Initiation* (London, 1960) 62, 128.

[9] Cf M. E. Boismard, *Quatre hymnes baptismales dans la première Epître de Pierre* (Paris, 1961).

[10] 'All these sayings [Mt 5, 38-48] contain something characteristic, new, reaching out beyond popular wisdom and piety and yet are in no sense specific to the scribes and rabbis or the Jewish apocalyptic. So here, if anywhere, we can find what is characteristic of the preaching of Jesus.' Rudolf Bultmann, *History of the Synoptic Tradition* (Oxford, 1963), 105.

[11] Cf K. Rahner, *Theological Investigations,* vol. IV, (London, 1966) 342: *The Hermeneutics of Eschatological Assertions:* 'Our basic thesis therefore is that from the present experience of salvation that the genuine future yet to come is known – as a preliminary outline helping us to understand properly the present'. J. Alfaro, *Escatología, herméneutica y lenguaje,* in *Salmaticensis* 25 (1980) 235: 'One can only speak significantly about the Christian *escaton*, in itself still hidden, if already in the present there are anticipatory signs of this 'ultimate' that is to come. Eschatological language cannot be other than the proleptic language of hope'.

[12] Cf K. Rahner, *The New Image of the Church* in *Theological Investigations,* X, (London, 1973) 7-12.

[13]On the theme of the rebuilding of the Church today, cf Paul VI, *Addresses at Wednesday Audiences*, from 7 July to 15 August 1976. Cf *Oss. Rom*. English edition, varia.

[14]Cf L. Bouyer, *op. cit.,* 60-77.

[15]'Christian brotherhood is not an ideal but a divine reality.' D. Bonhoeffer, *Life Together* (London, 1964) 15; 'Innumerable times a whole Christian community has broken down because it had sprung from a wish-dream' (*ibid*). 'Only that fellowship which faces such disillusionment, with all its unhappy and ugly aspects, begins to be what it should be in God's sight, begins to grasp in faith the promise that is given to it. The sooner this shock of disillusionment comes to an individual and to a community the better for both' (*ibid*). 'One who wants more than what Christ has established does not want Christian brotherhood. He is looking for some extraordinary social experience which he has not found elsewhere; he is bringing muddled and impure desires to the Christian brotherhood' (p. 14). He who goes after this 'more' is refusing to accept in the community the humble and poor face of Jesus; he becomes demanding with God, with his neighbour and with himself in a tiring and dangerous way.

[16]Cf G. Zevini, *Attualizzazione della parola di Dio nella comunità e nei gruppi ecclesiali* in *Attualizzazione della parola di Dio nelle nostre comunità* (Bologna, 1983) 205-32, esp. 217-23; F. Voltaggio, *La Parola di Dio nelle Comunità Neo-Catecumenali* in G. Zevini, *Incontro con la Bibbia. Leggere, pregare, annunziare* (Roma, 1978) 187-91; Y. Congar, *Tradition and Traditions* (London, 1966) 338-346.

[17]'Although incomplete and in need of deeper in

vestigations and further enrichment, the said evaluation (of negative and positive aspects in the diverse Christian communities in the Spanish Church) can be, for the moment, a point of reference sufficiently objective and extensive... Deliberately we present anthropological, sociological and ecclesial questions mixed together, granted that that is how they appear to the eyes of an observer of the life of these small communities' (*Servicio pastoral a las Pequeñas Comunidades Cristianas, Documento de la Comisión Episcopal de Pastoral,* in *Ecclesia,* 2073 [10-17 April 1982] 11, 19).

[18]Cf *Lumen Gentium,* 33, and *Apostolicam Actuositatem,* 15-22. G. Philips comments on number 33: 'Besides this mission which corresponds to all lay people without distinction, there exists for *some of them a special vocation* which puts them more directly at the service of the hierarchy. However strange it may seem the terrain here is sown with traps; nonetheless the existence of such a vocation, linked without any doubt to the charismatic area, cannot be disputed' (*L'Eglise et son mystère au IIe Concile du Vatican. Histoire, texte et commentaire de la Constitution Lumen Gentium,* II, [Louvain 1968] 28). Author's emphasis.

Cf A. Laurentin/M. Dujarier, *Catéchumenat. Donné de l'histoire et perspectives nouvelles* (Paris, 1969 - Collection Vivante Liturgie, 83); C. Florisn, *El catecumenado* (Madrid, 1972); M. Dujarier, *Brève histoire du Catéchumenat* (Abidjan, 1980) and *A History of the Catechumenate* (New York, 1979); D. Borobio, *ecumenado* in C. Floristan-J.J. Tamayo, ed, *ceptos Fundamentales de Pastoral* (Madrid,), 99-120. In the *Rite for the Christian Initia-*

tion of Adults (London, 1987) certain aspects were specified on the basis of a question raised by the Neo-Catechumenal Communities, cf A. Bugnini, *La riforma liturgica, 1948-1975* (Rome, 1983) 579. Balthasar Fischer, in his study of the *Ordo Initiationis Christianae Adultorum*, in reference to chapter IV, writes: 'Much more important and of greater pastoral significance is chapter IV, which bears the long title: *De praeparandis ad confirmationem et eucharistiam adultis qui, infantes baptizati, catechesim non receperunt.* From the pastoral indications contained in the eleven paragraphs (295-305), impetus has been derived, since the appearance of the *Ordo,* for a movement of supreme importance, operating worldwide, and working for the recovery of those far from the Church: the so-called Neo-Catechumenate. This leads by means of a way of faith analagous to that by which, according to our *Ordo,* the non-baptised travels, someone who, while Christian in name by virtue of his baptism, wishes under the impulse of the Holy Spirit to become so definitively in fact' (Balthasar Fischer, *Die Struktur des Ordo Initiationis Christianae Adultorum von 1972* in *Liturgia opera divina e umana. Studi sulla riforma liturgica offerti a S. E. Mons Annibale Bugnini in occasione del suo 70° compleanno,* edited by P. Jounel, R. Kaczynski and G. Pasqualetti [Rome, 1982] 375-385).

[20]Cf *Oss. Rom.*, 5-6 April 1983.

[21]Cf *Lumen Gentium,* 26 (quoting a prayer from the Spanish Mozarabic Rite).

[22]X. Léon-Dufour, *Dictionary of Biblical Theology* (London, 1967).

[23]H. de Lubac, *Christian faith: structure of the*

Apostles Creed, (London, 1986) 72: 'Personal faith is at the same time of absolute necessity as belief. It is not to remain formal and empty, if it is to exist at all, it must be nourished by this belief. It presupposes, integrates and unites it, making it share its own personal character.' Faith is not simply a leaning on God or an act of trust in him, without also consenting to the history of salvation professed in the Creed. Cf also J.H. Newman, *Grammar of Assent* (London, 1870; New York, 1955) 93-94: 'We are now able to determine what a dogma of faith is, and what it is to believe in. A dogma is a proposition; it stands for a notion or a thing; and to believe it is to give the assent of the mind to it, as it stands for the one or the other. To give a real assent to it is an act of religion; to give a notional, is a theological act. It is discerned, rested in, and appropriated as a reality, by the religious imagination; it is held as a truth, by the theological intellect. Not as if there were, in fact, or could be, any line of demarcation or party-wall between these two modes of assent, the religious and the theological. (...) There is a theological habit of mind and a religious, each distinct from each, religion using theology and theology using religion. (...) Faith, in its theological sense, includes a belief, not only in the thing believed, but also in the ground of believing; that is, not only belief in certain doctrines, but belief in them expressly because God has revealed them.'

[24] Cf *Confessions of St Augustine*, VIII, 2.

[25] Cf St Basil, *De Spiritu Sancto,* XXV, 36; PG 32, 132 B. The hypothesis is not farfetched which suggests that the words of the introduction to the 'Our Father', in the Eucharistic celebration of the Roman Rite, 'divina institutione formati', instead

of a parallel expression to 'praeceptis salutaribus moniti', refer to baptism, as a reality which makes man son of God. O. Rousseau, *Le 'Pater' dans la liturgie de la messe* in *Cours et Conferences,* VII (Louvain, 1929) 231-241; on p. 235 he is inclined to see the origin of the reference to 'audemus dicere' in the practice of the Catechumenate, particularly in the East); J. A. Jungmann, *The Mass of the Roman Rite* (Missarum Sollemnia), II (New York, 1959) 465; S. Sabugal, *El Padre Nuestro en la interpretación catequetica antigua y moderna* (Salamanca, 1982).

[26]So far (1986), a few communities have finished the Neo-Catechumenal Way by renewing their baptismal promises: the first communities in Rome from the parishes of the Canadian Martyrs and St Francesca Cabrini and the first communities in Madrid.

[27]Part of a statement issued by the first community of the Canadian Martyrs parish in Rome, and included in a booklet entitled *Il Neo-Catecumenato. Un'esperienza di evangelizzazione e catechesi in atto in questa generazione. Sintesi delle sue linee di fondo.* An English translation was made, but is now out of print.

[28]For example, one can see how much these two Popes have said in various official audiences or in visitations of parishes where the Neo-Catechumenal Way is established. We confine ourselves here to the most important. PAUL VI: General Audience, 8 May 1974 (cf *Notitiae,* 95-96 [July-August 1974] 228-30); General Audience, 12 January 1977 (cf *Oss. Rom.,* 7-8 January 1977). JOHN PAUL II: Visitation of the Canadian Martyrs' parish, 2 November 1980 (*Oss. Rom.,* 3-4 November 1980); Private Audience for itinerant catechists, 7 January 1982 (*Oss. Rom.,* 7-8 January 1982, English ed.

15 February 1982); General Audience addressing priests taking part in a meeting on 'Penance and Reconciliation' organised by Neo-Catechumenal communities, 10 Feb 1983 (*Oss. Rom.,* 11 February 1983), plus his words at the Angelus on Sunday, 13 February (*Oss. Rom.,* 14-15 February 1983). We note in passing that during these years Pope John Paul II, while on pastoral visitation to the parishes of his diocese, has met the Neo-Catechumenal communities on more than twenty occasions, and always responding with words of encouragement. Most recently, on 31 January 1988, in the parish of St Maria Goretti (*Oss. Rom.,* 1-2 February 1988), the Pope confirmed his approval of this Way as coherent with the nature of the parish as such, and as offering an effective witness to the tired and de-Christianised historical context of the Church, especially in Europe.

[29]Cf Pope John Paul II, *The Way of the New Man* (a speech given to Neo-Catechumenal communities of the parish of the Canadian Martyrs), originally published in *Oss. Rom.,* 3-4 November 1980. An indexed collection of this and all other speeches up to the last referred has now been published in English by the Neo-Catechumenal Centre in Rome: *The Neo-Catechumenal Way in the discourses of Paul VI and John Paul II* (pro manuscripto), Rome 1987.

[30]*Oss. Rom.,* 12 October 1985; English edition 21 October 1985. The Pope, in the conclusion to his address, indicated the conditions 'to achieve an effective work of evangelisation', conditions which are at the same time criteria of discernment to recognise and identify an authentic work of evangelisation: a) return to the 'very first apostolic model'; b) 'where we see that fruits of life are

given'; c) 'where the Church, like Mary, is venerated and welcomed (listened to) as a Mother'. It is worth noting that these are precisely the elements that one recognises in the experience of evangelisation of the Neo-Catechumenal communities, particularly in the work of the itinerants.

[31]Final Report of the Second Plenary Assembly of the Extraordinary Synod of Bishops, II, B, 2 (*Oss. Rom.*, 10 December 1985; English translation published in *Briefing*, XV, 24 [1985] for the Bishops' Conference of England and Wales).

[32]Y. Congar, referring to chapter IV, i, of the Constitution *Gaudium et Spes* of the Second Vatican Council, which has as its title: '*Mission* of the Church in the modern world', has written: "To tell the truth, the first responsibility of the Church with regard to the world is to convert it to the Gospel... It is thus that the world will convert to the Church. However, there is another area of mission for the Church, another activity of the Church in respect of the world, which she exercises in and upon the world *in its worldly structures and activity*, when it moves within the world's own order. This is the ambience, the activity which *Gaudium et Spes* is looking at... It is not possible to separate, in the Church's exercise of her mission, the goal of human well-being and the preaching of the Gospel.' (*El Papel de la Iglesia en el mundo de Hoy* in *La Iglesia en el mundo de hoy* [Madrid, 1970] 373f).

[33]The theological problem of evil becomes even more acute in terms of the cross of Jesus as the consequence of sin; however, in this infinite radicality there is also enlightenment: 'The problem of man's sin is transformed into the mystery – or the scandal – of the love of God.' (W. Kern, *Übel*.

in *Lexicon für Theologie und Kirche,* X [Freiburg i.B., 1966] col. 434). In the cross of Jesus and in the cross of the personal history of every human being, paradoxically, God has shown his love.

BIBLIOGRAPHY

ARGUELLO F. (Kiko), *Le Communità Neo-Catecumenali* in *Rivista di vita spirituale* 2 (1975) 191ff.

ID. *Il convegno dei parroci delle Comunità Neo-Catecumenali in vista del Sinodo su 'La catechesi nel nostro tempo', Roma, 10-13 gennaio 1977* (pro manuscripto), especially 103-127: *Catechesi sul Cammino Neo-Catecumenale.*

ID. *Il Neo-Catecumenato. Un'esperienza di evangelizzazione e catechesi in atto in questa generazione. Sintesi delle sue linee di fondo* in *Rivista di vita spirituale* 1 (1977) 98ff.

ID. *Address of Kiko Arguello to the Plenary Assembly of the Sacred Congregation for the Evangelisation of the Peoples* (pro manuscripto), Neo-Catechumenal Centre of Rome.

ID. *Brief intervention by Kiko Arguello on the Neo-Catechumenal Way to the Assembly of the Synod of Bishops meeting on Penance and Reconciliation,* 21 October 1983.

DELLA TORRE L., *Le Comunità Neo-Catecumenali* in *Rivista di Pastorale liturgica* 48 (1971) 512-515.

ID., *Il Neo-Catecumenato,* in *Communio* 32 (1977) 58-88.

FAVALE A., *Movimenti ecclesiali* (IV: *Comunità Neo-Catecumenali)* in S. DE FLORES - S. MEO, ed., *Nuovo Dizionario di Mariologia,* (Roma, 1985) 965-968.

GIUDICE E., *Il Neo-Catecumenato: cammino di rievangelizzazione per i lontani (itinerario di riiniziazione cristiana per adulti)* (Roma, 1985-1986).

GRASSO L., *Le Comunità Neo-Catecumenali* in *Rivista di pastorale liturgica* 16 (1978) 20-22.

HUGUERAS J., *Comunidades Neo-Catecumenales en la parroquia de S. Pedro el Real ("La Paloma") de Madrid,* in *Evangelización y hombre de hoy. Congreso,* (Madrid, 1986) 325-330.

LAU ENGELS, *Der Neo-Katechumenat* in *Liturgisches Jahrbuch,* 29 (1979) 180-185.

VOLTAGGIO F., *La parola di Dio nelle Comunità Neo-Catecumenali* in G ZEVINI, ed., *Incontro con la Bibbia. Leggere, pregare, annunziare* (Roma, 1978) 187-191.

ZEVINI G., *Le Comunità Neo-Catecumenali. Una pastorale di evangelizzazione permanente* in A. AMATO, ed., *Temi teologici-pastorali* (Roma, 1977) 103-125.

ID., *The Christian Initiation of Adults into the Neo-Catechumenal Community* in *Concilium* 2 (1979) 65-74.

ID., *Neo-Catecumenato,* in S. DE FIORES - T. GOFFI, ed., *Nuovo Dizionario di Spiritualità* (Roma, 1979) 1056-1073.

ID., *Il Cammino Neo-Catecumenale. Itinerario di maturazione nella fede* in A. FAVALE, ed., *Movimenti ecclesiali contemporanei. Dimensioni storiche, teologico-spirituali ed apostoliche* (Roma, 1982) 231-267.

Cf also:

NOTITIAE 85 (1973) 280ff.
ID., 10 (1974) 228-230